T0062439

Turfloop: Conscious Pariah

How the University of the North
brought in the Age of Barack Obama
beyond our Wildest Dreams

Edited by Chris Kanyane

Order this book online at www.trafford.com
or email orders@trafford.com

Most Trafford titles are also available at major online book retailers.

© Copyright 2010 Chris Kanyane.
All rights reserved. No part of this publication may be reproduced, stored
in a retrieval system, or transmitted, in any form or by any means, electronic,
mechanical, photocopying, recording, or otherwise, without
the written prior permission of the author.

Printed in Victoria, BC, Canada.

ISBN: 978-1-4269-2461-3

*Our mission is to efficiently provide the world's finest, most
comprehensive book publishing service, enabling every author to
experience success. To find out how to publish your book, your way, and
have it available worldwide, visit us online at www.trafford.com*

Trafford rev. 01/04/2010

 www.trafford.com

North America & international
toll-free: 1 888 232 4444 (USA & Canada)
phone: 250 383 6864 ♦ fax: 812 355 4082

Contents

Preface

We have approached this book about the University of the North like detectives genuinely curious about the evolution of African advancement and culture. Before we get on with our detective work we would like to reflect on scientific developments that provides a context on what we are about to describe and discuss:

It is because of Isaac Newton and Rene Descartes that Western culture is steeped in the superstition of materialism. The superstition of materialism says that what we experience through the five senses is the only valid test of reality. Not only do my five senses give me information; they are also extremely reliable.

Experience shows that this is not true. After all, our senses tell us that the earth is flat. My senses tell me that the ground I walk on is stationary, but it is spinning at a dizzying speed and hurdling through space at thousands of miles an hour.

What we are trying to put forward here is that the truth might not be the truth. Your truth may be your response to your observation and have nothing to do with the actual truth. The human eye can only see between 370 to 500 billions of meters but for practical purposes this is far fetched. A dog will hear sounds and, smell odors that people cannot.

What we experience in the physical world is just a lens of perception giving us a very distorted and fragmented view of something that is much vaster and abstract.

So the question is what is the real nature of the world? Because what we are seeing, touching, tasting and smelling is the response of our flawed senses.

What are the real truths about University of the North during the 1960s, 1970s and the 1980s, popularly known as Turfloop? Before we answer this question let us answer the earlier one that we posed about what is the nature of the world:

In this world is flowing quantum soup. We take that quantum soup, which is a field of infinite possibility in a continuum of the present and freeze it into an object of material physical perceptions that is fixed in space and time.

Sir John Heckels, who won the Nobel Peace Prize in physiology and medicine once said, *I want you to know that there are no ugliness in the real world.* In the act of perception we take the field of infinite possibilities – this huge ineffable abstract nothingness – and create ideas which control us. The tragic thing is that we do this within the boundaries of our own preconceived notions of how things should be. For example, some books claim that what happened at the University of the North (popularly knows as Turfloop) from the 1960s to the 1980s was unrest and resistance politics.

This might have nothing to do with the real truth. It might be just a dogma.
But let us answer the question about the real nature of the world. Dr. Ellen Langer wrote a book called *Mindfulness* in which she describes an experiment with 100 80-year olds. She took these octogenarians to a monastery outside Boston in which she created a sensory reach environment from the 1950s. She played Elvis Presley records and broadcasts of Walter Cronkite reading the news. Langer instructed the 80-year olds to be as they had been in the 1950s.

After three weeks, all of the participants in the experiment had reversed the biological marks of aging: their visual threshold changed, their skin became more elastic and soft, their wrinkles disappeared, their bone density changed, their adrenalin levels were higher. Biologically, they became several years younger. All Langer had done was recreate an environment in with the participants had been young and told them to be the way that they had been then.

So what we call reality is nothing other than a socially programmed hypnosis or an induced fiction that we create and participate in.

We argue in this book how that Turfloop was the centre and model giving inspiration to the whole of South Africa that eventually ushering in the the brand new world which we call the Age of Barack Obama.

Introduction:

The Age of Barack Obama

Barack Obama's ascension to the presidency of the United States of America is symbolic. Its symbolic nature does not derive from Obama's race as many tell us; it derives from the lesson that we have reached the age of change. Further, it signals the emergence of a brand new world.

Obama embodies change. His youthfulness attests to the fact that he is representative of the progressives who would bring to bear policies that represent the current and indeed future trend of the world. Obama is in the best position to lay the foundation of an America that will continue to lead the world in creating a better society. This seems to be a fact that the entire American citizenry have embraced. It seems that Americans, having gotten tired of the same clique of leaders who perpetrate the same policies, in the same drab way, have decided to pitch tents with somebody who offers them the change they can believe in.

Obama represent the age of inclusion. His are politics of invitation that gives hope to the young, to the old, and to the middle aged progressives. His campaign offered a

"WE-alliance." He didn't flaunt experience or perfection; he didn't beg for pity by harping on the race issue. He presented himself from the very beginning as a native son who has come to guide the affairs of his country through uncertain terrain. And indeed he feels—as do we-- that he is best qualified to steer the ship of state through the dark waters of the future because he epitomizes change in its most progressive form.

Obama's election is not just a victory for Blacks. It is a victory for all. Even so, the Obama victory means more to the African-American community.

And then there is Africa. The last time a single event had this much impact on the continent was in 1957, when Ghana gained independence. Nkrumah's Ghana was a land of hope and possibility for all Africans. Africa came alive. This was the period before the false promises and the false hopes. We know how Ghana and every other African country turned out. Obama's triumph is making Africans feel whole and alive again. In spite of the pitiful condition of the continent, the Obama victory reminds Africans of that era of irrational exuberance and irrational optimism.

With the coming of Barack Obama, Africans are looking to Washington DC. Unfortunately, nothing extraordinary will take place in or towards the African continent. Although Barack Obama's father was Kenyan, he will quickly sign an order to bomb Kenya if it is in the American interest. This means that whatever change that is going to take place and take hold in Africa must come from Africans themselves.

As president of the United States, Obama's mandate is to protect and advance the national interest of his country. Beyond that, he will look to Europe, Asia, Latin America, and the Middle East. Africa will be an afterthought, as it always has been. Maybe then Africans will realize that their destiny is in their own hands.

Chapter 1:

The Idea of a University for Africans

Higher education for Blacks in South Africa dates to 1916 with the establishment of the African Native College.

Until 1960, universities in South Africa fell into two categories: the English language universities of Cape Town, the Witwatersrand, Natal and Rhodes; and the Afrikaans language universities of Pretoria, Stellenbosch, Potchestroom, and the Free State. The University of South Africa was unique in that it was the only distance education university which offered instruction in both English and Afrikaans. Students of all races could register without violating the apartheid policy of strict racial segregation.

Apart from the medium of instruction, the universities were governed by two fundamentally different philosophies. The English language universities emphasized the supreme importance of academic freedom and academic autonomy. They maintained that the university should select its students on no grounds other than academic ones. They contended that the university should be free to administer its own courses, syllabi, curricula, and examinations without reference to external authority.

The Afrikaans language universities insisted that the university be compelled to conform to national policy and social order. The primary aim of the university, according to this philosophy, was to serve its community. This is enshrined in Article 14 of the Christian-National Education Manifesto of 1948 which said: *with regard to the national principle, we believe that the coloured man can be made race conscious if the principle of apartheid is strictly applied in education...,*

The different in approach can be traced to the cultural backgrounds of the two language groups. Whilst the English language universities, true to their liberal tradition, opened their doors to non white students, the Afrikaans universities were closed to people of colour – apparently in defense of ethnic purity.

Of particular interest was that in that great debate on the nature of the university, the black perspective had no forum. Even in the liberal English universities where few non whites students were found they were psychological conguered and could do nothing to raise their concerns, theirs were to go to the lecture room sit down and take notes. Nelson Mandela recalled that even in the lecture rooms, white students would move if a black student sat near them. The environment in the English universities reminded all non whites that they were not part of the university community.

Towards the middle of the 1950s it was felt that the number of universities for Black students should be increased, so in 1959 the Parliament of the Union of South Africa passed the Extension of University Education Act. The Act established two additional university colleges for Blacks, one for coloureds and one for Indians.

The University College of the North was founded on 1 August, 1959, as a to serve the Northern Sotho, Southern Sotho, Tsonga, Tswana and Venda ethnic communities. However, the University has on occasion accepted students from South West Africa (Namibia), Zimbabwe and Malawi.

The establishment of ethnic universities should be viewed against the apartheid policy of ,"separate development," South Africa's white, coloured, Asian and the eight Bantu nations were called separate nations. Every aspect of life was dominated by the thought: to what group does that man belong? The universities that were created by the University Act of 1959 were meant to prepare their graduates for future participation in the development of their ethnic communities.

The first council of the University of the North was appointed on 14 August 1959 and its first advisory council on 1 January 1960. The first senate was constituted in September, 1960 and met for the first time on 13 October.

The members of the council of the University were whites, appointed by the Minister of Bantu Education. The advisory council was composed entirely of non whites but controlled by whites. According to official policy, this arrangement was for the good of the non white and there was a promise that the University would be handed over to the non whites as soon as they were *ready,* to manage the University.

Parliament stipulated at the inception of the University College of the North that the institution should fall under the academic trusteeship of the University of South Africa. This relationship functioned reasonably well, but gradually it became evident that the university college would be able to do justice to its own unique character and realize its ideals only if it could develop on its own. Thus in 1969, the Republic of South Africa Parliament made provision for the academic independence through the University of the North Act (Act No. 47 of 1969), and on 1 January, 1970, the decade-long relationship with the University of South Africa was dissolved, and the University of the North came into being.

The first Black rector and Principal (Professor WM Kgware) of any university in South Africa was appointed to the University of the North on 1 January 1977. Thus University of the North provided the ideological leadership for other Black universities in South Africa and in neighboring countries. The appointment of Kgware was spearheaded by what would later become known as the Turfloop testimony.

The Council of the University was reconstituted on 1 January, 1978. This was also a result of Turfloop testimony. The Turfloop Testimony ideals were soon to spread through townships and villages.

At the same time the University Council was reconstituted, the predominantly black Advisory Council was abolished – again in the spirit of the Turfloop Testimony. A vice rector was installed.

The first rector of the university was Prof E.F Potgieter, a white Afrikaner from Pretoria.

What follows is his account of the establishment of the university and of his ideals for the university as a founding Rector and principal.

A Few Memories of the First Rector of the University of the North

Never shall I forget the day I travelled with my family to the land of the Mamabolo where I had undertaken to begin another University in South Africa.

There was virtually nothing there, and some newspaper referred to this new university as a still-born baby. To this remark, I responded by admitting that the baby was still being born. This I said to such men as Kgware, Ntsanwisi, Lekhela, Van Dyk, Galloway and others. We were not many at that stage, but some of the first students are today prominent men.

Never shall I forget the day when I asked the White builder to hurry up and build the Chemistry laboratory. He wanted to know what authority I had to tell him to get a move on. When I informed him that I was the Principal of this new University, he wryly commented, "That will be the day."

But this was not the grand finale. The then Minister of Foreign Affairs decided that he wished to bring the Right Honourable Sir Harold Macmillan, the then Prime Minister of Great Britain, to have a look at the University that I was still trying to get built. The Prime Minister eventually came to the University guarded by Scotland Yard personnel, followed by RSA Security personnel. Never shall I forget the sympathy in his eyes when I told him that we were still in the process of building. He had sympathy on me because there was no staff and also there were no students.

Only after the British Prime Minister had visited did staff and students arrive. Once I received a remarkable application for admission to the University. It read more or less as follows:

Having passed Standard 6 by virtue of my brilliant brain, I now apply for admission for admission to your institution to be trained in bricklaying and lorry-driving.

I wish I had kept this letter!

During those early times a section of the press did not help us in our task. One foreign correspondent once asked me, with a supercilious smile, whether I could show him the thatched huts and theological foundation of this University I was building. With the aid of Black staff members I showed him, and he left in shameful confusion.

This sort of people made me weary. One day whilst I was preparing a lawn in front of my house, a car stopped, a man got out of the car, pointed at my house and wanted to know from me whether the Rector and Principal of the University was around. In great honesty, I told him, also pointing to the house, that he certainly was not there. The man drove off, and I returned sweating to the leveling of the garden.

But help for our task did come from other sources. For instance, the late Chief Mamabolo arrived at my house one night. His servants were driving two black oxen. Chief Mamabolo thanked me for having started the University in this part of the world and gave me the two black oxen, he then left. I still feel sorry for myself, trying that night to find a safe place for the black oxen in the black of the night. The next morning I sold them to a local butcher and banked the proceeds for the University.

At this stage I had formulated my message for the staff. These staff members were Black and White. My message was a simple one: *Let us work for five years and then talk.*

But in between these incidents and the work, I had to find a means of relaxation. So I returned to the things I knew. Simple things – horses and hunting. In the direction of Lekganyane, Mamabolo, Sandsloot, further north I rode, stabling the horses near my home.

One night I brought a dead lion which I had shot in the Venda area back to my house. The next morning I was obliged to lure the horses back to their stable with sugar, because they had apparently thought that the Devil himself had come to their doorstep.

As a member of the Akademie veir Wetenskap en Kuns; as a member of the Council of the University of South Africa; as an Officer in the Defence Force of our Fatherland; with many Black friends in the veld who had risked their lives with me, I am proud to say that the University of the North shall always stir a chord in my heart, especially when the stirring is caused by leaders, born and bred there – students who entered the University of Life thereafter and are still complying with its more difficult syllabus.

A final thought on the Field Marshal Montgomery of Alamein, who also visited the University. It was by that time functioning as a University when I asked him what his life's formula was, he stated in simple terms that he did not like a person who sat behind him – as though he intended to stab him in the back. Those who were present will well remember that I stood up and went and sat in the front row of the audience, proving to him that I was no traitor.

Reminiscences of the Second Rector and Principal of the University of the North Dr BT Boshoff

On the first of December 1969 I entered the expensively carpeted and beautifully paneled office of the Rector and Principal of the University College of the North – the university college destined to become within a few weeks the University of the North. Having heard while I was still in Pretoria a wide variety of opinions purported to have been expressed by members of the staff, both White and Black, and even some students, of how soon the new Rector will have to resign and go back to the job he knows, I believe that I sat down on the Rector's chair with some misgivings, wondering what I had let myself in for.

Why I had the audacity to accept the post was not difficult to determine. I was appointed Deputy Secretary for the Department of Bantu Education, in the previous year. It very soon became clear to me that as Secretary of Education in the Transkei I had outgrown the head office atmosphere of Bantu Education, and the Rectorship of the University came as a relief from a situation that had the makings of confrontation.

One of the very first persons to welcome me in my office was Professor Kgware. I immediately came into contact with the very sensitive situation the University for Blacks had – and I believe still has—to deal with. In due course tea was served … in two different cups; one was of beautiful bone china, while the other was thick, glazed earthenware specimen. Fortunately I was in a position to take the earthenware cup, leaving the other for my visitor. I wonder whether Professor Kgware still remembers the incident. Fortunately I had set aside that way of doing things many years before. Now I think it is the time to laugh at those traditional ways of doing things that a white person should sip tea from a beautiful cup while the black person sip his tea from thick ugly earthenware cup.

However there I was, Rector and Principal of a college in the bush. I very soon discovered an amazing paradox. Many people, including some academics who had been so highly critical of the establishment of the University, and who were responsible for coining the term, *college in the bush,* were showing signs of coming around to recognize and to accept the University as a University – thanks to the great work that was done by my predecessor Professor ET Potgieter and members of staff. On the other hand – in some quarters – impeccable supporters of the government policy were rather slow in ceding this recognition. Please note .. some quarters not all.

I have on my desk my visitors' book and paging it through and reading the names of the many people that passed through my office, I am extremely grateful for the wonderful opportunity I had by virtue of the Rectorship of the University of the North. Looking at South Africa through the eyes of very intelligent and correctly informed visitors from abroad. One of them, who at the time of his visit was the Dean of Balliol College, Oxford, and who was guest of the University of the Witwatersrand exclaimed: But you are not managing a University. You are managing the affairs of your country! How right he was.

The relationship with the students was always difficult. No doubt there were reasons, but I believe that one of the more important reasons was explained to me one Saturday morning on my way to Polokwane. I always gave students lifts into town. On this occasion I was dressed in shorts, in my private car and on my way to the golf course. I lifted four students. I must explain that they were first-year students who had just arrived. The incident occurred before the official opening of the University that year.

After usual greetings I asked, Do you know who I am?
No, – came the reply.

Well I am the Rector, Professor Boshoff.
Silence. In the rear-view mirror I saw surprise on the faces
of the three of them sitting at the back.

Are you surprised that I am the Rector?
I can see that you are surprised. Why are you surprised?
Silence.

I continued the conversation with the students: Are
you willing to tell me why are you surprised? You never
expected the Rector to give you a lift?"

The student sitting next to me had by then overcome
his suspicious and began to talk freely and openly. He
told me that his parents lived in Soweto that he had
arrived at the University with fear in his heart because
of what he had been told about the University and the
Rector. His friends agreed with him. One also came
from Soweto, the other from Garankuwa, and the
fourth from Kimberly.

I realized then that we were fighting a losing battle –
unless, to use the modern phraseology, we were willing
to bury the holy cows…one of them being the notion
that God had given us special task of doing good to the
Blacks, providing laws to compel them to accept the
good things we did for them – such as providing them
with their own University!

Statement of Nelson Mandela, the President of the African National Congress, on the Occasion of His Installation as the Chancellor of the University of the North at the Congregation of the University.

25 April 1992

Comrades and friends:

It is an immutable fact of life that no power on earth can shackle the human spirit forever. However, this universal truth, that has permeated the social fabric of society from time immemorial and having been passed on from generation to generation, seem to still elude many, even as we move towards the end of the twentieth century. The infamous apartheid system has created artificial inducements, has built up an elaborate system of social engineering in terms of which black education at a tertiary level has been fragmented and people allocated to universities on the basis of race and tribe. The creation of the bush universities was but one way in which government tries to exclude the black majority from the mainstream universities.

It is not the irony of history that today I stand here before you to be installed as the chancellor of the University of the North.

The fact that both this university and I have reached this point through the narrow path of fire - characterised by relentless struggle. We have converged on this summit of victory after many sacrifices. In this regard, it is instructive to recall that Turfloop was established at the time when many freedom fighters were being herded into prisons, whilst others were forced to take sanctuary in the relative safety of foreign lands. At the time, architects of our misery believed themselves to have succeeded in defying the law of nature - they were convinced that the human spirit in us was broken forever. Three decades later, the corpse of apartheid lies prostrate at the feet of people's power.

However, our journey to this point has never been an easy one. We literally had to walk through a garden of thorns, and we are still wading across rivers of blood. It is a matter of great pride to us that, this university, like many others did not become an institution of servitude as was the design of our oppressors. In this regard, we must single out the heroic role of the students and commend them highly for their commitment to the struggle. The indelible history of the struggle of the students on this campus is full of events of indomitable courage and resilience. Students like Onkgopotse Tiro, Fistus Mothudi, Ignitius Mathebule and many others inscribed the name of Turfloop on the conscience of our people. That Turfloop is today counted in the roll of honour is because of their valiant deeds. These heroes and heroines of our people are no more today. May we observe a moment of silence in memory of all the martyrs of our university.

Thank you.

Mr. Chairman of Council
On this campus, our students organised a Pro-Frelimo rally simultaneously with a much bigger rally at Curries Fountain in Durban in the wake of the victory of the national liberation struggle against Portuguese colonialism.

Taking place as it did, at a time when the apartheid rule held sway, that rally was a truly remarkable expression of international solidarity with forces of freedom. It became a standard bearer - an acid test, against which efforts by successive generation of students, on this campus and elsewhere would be pitted.

Our students proved to be more than equal to the task. Their tenacity became an unprecedented phenomenon. This is the reason why our campus had to be occupied by the army, for a period of no less than three years in the 1980s. Even as we speak, the army continues to man a military post on a hill-top not far from here. It is little wonder, therefore, that Turfloop has produced national leaders of the stature of Cyril Ramaphosa, Phandelani Nevolovhodwe, Frank Chikane and many others. I am, therefore, deeply honoured and humbled to be associated with an institution which has rendered such outstanding service to this our beloved country. Accordingly, I accept this chancellorship with all humility.

It must be said, that in recent time, the governing bodies of this university have shown a marked readiness to initiate changes intended to transform the university in response to the winds of change blowing across the length and breadth of country. The appointment of Professor Chabani Manganyi as vice chancellor and principal of the university, and today my installation as chancellor, are, amongst others, developments which bear eloquent testimony to the new spirit of transformation reigning supreme on these hills of Turfloop. I wish to take this opportunity to congratulate Professor Manganyi on a job exceedingly well done. Within a very short space of time, he has succeeded to steer our institution towards a new beginning, and thus we are on course to being a true people's university. At last, we are transforming an instrument of oppression into a vehicle of liberation.

Mr. Chairman of Council

As we enter the still waters of transformation we must brace ourselves for the inevitable undercurrent. The creation of a new society has never been an easy one. On that plane, we have to make a clean and at time painful break, with tradition and the things to which we are accustomed. Those who seek to rely on old landmarks in their quest for a new society will find themselves wandering aimlessly in a hostile jungle. Yesterday's familiar terrain is disappearing before our very eyes. We are, being thrust into the role of pioneers and torch bearers into a new and democratic South Africa. It is us whom history has charged, with the task of opening up new realms, to unveil the hitherto hidden horizons, so that the coming generations can live in a land where merit is the only determinant of success.

We are distressed to note that our compatriots in the National Party still have such grave reservations about democracy. While State President de Klerk and his party pay lip service to this concept, it is clear from his speech of 23rd April that he and his colleagues are not prepared to accept the rhetorical frills with which de Klerk adorns the National Party's proposals, it is evident that what they really seek is the continued incumbency of the National Party even in the event that it loses an election.

It is the National Party's stubborn refusal to give up exclusive power that constitutes the primary stumbling block to the success of Codesa.

The ANC would like Codesa ll to be more than a mere talking shop for the repetition of comfortable platitudes. It must be an occasion when concrete decision affecting the future of our country can be agreed upon. The sense of urgency that informs the constituencies we represent is clearly absent in the case of the national party. South Africa has waited too long for change. We are, consequently, very impatient and the National Party can no longer equivocate on this matter.

No party, to our knowledge, has thus far put forward a winner takes all solution. On the contrary, it is the National Party that is advocating a loser takes all solution which is unprecedented in any democracy. In other words what South Africa is being asked to accept is a constitutional dispensation that will permit the political parties to ignore the verdict of the electorate.

Speaking plainly, the National Party wants to retain its hand on the levers of power even when after a democratic election has demonstrated that it does not enjoy the confidence of the South African electorate.

The National Party's desire to cling to power at all costs emerges even more sharply in the government's proposals for the transition. Our concern here is not the labels that politicians stick on their wares but the actual substance of their proposals. De Klerk's claim that his proposals are intended to avoid the temptations of absolute power is disingenuous. If accepted, the outcome will not be an interim government that enjoys the confidence of the majority of South Africans, but a slightly refurbished National Party government. The ANC also rejects outright the suggestion that elections be held to constitute an executive council. Our position remains unchanged. We call for elections for a constituent assembly which shall also have legislative powers while a new constitution is being negotiated.

De Klerk's veiled threat to unilaterally outlaw Umkhonto we Sizwe is known . As far as the ANC is concerned we have scrupulously avoided engaging in public debate on this issue because it is the subject of extremely sensitive bilateral negotiations between the government and ourselves. The government has constantly made provocative remarks on the subject which require us to respond.

Firstly, it has to be clearly understood that Umkhonto we Sizwe is not a private army but an insurgent army created by the national liberation movement to rid our country of the crime of apartheid. Umkhonto we Sizwe is recognised as a legitimate military formation in international law and in terms of the Geneva agreements. Government attempts to act unilaterally on this matter pose as grave a threat to our bilateral negotiations as their intransigence poses to the entire process set in motion by Codesa.

The ANC will not disband Umkhonto we Sizwe. But we are equally determined that the de Klerk government will not wreck the negotiations with ill-conceived bombast and reckless behaviour.

Mr. Chairman of Council,

Change is as unsettling as it is painful. It cannot be any different because change is movement - a tension caused by contradictions which are part of existence. At times of momentous developments, when societies reach their own high noon, everything else becomes uncertain except for the golden gate that must be reached - the goal of freedom. Like our wider society out there, our university is at a crossroads.

We are, therefore, being called upon to be firm in our convictions, yet very accommodating and flexible in our approach. Yes, we are bound to hurt ourselves in the process, but if we are sensitive and careful enough, we shall be able to heal our wounds and rise again. Only this time, we shall be the wiser and, therefore, much stronger. Lest we lose heart, our cherished goal of freedom for all, now looms large on the horizon. This must reinforce our will to do good to those whom we lead as well as our nation.

We are beginning to experiment with the future. Contradictions must consequently abound.

Growing pains, what unites us, that which cements us together into a solid whole, is our common goal of education for the youth of the motherland. It is this priceless objective - far nobler than our imagining, which must never be sacrificed on the altar of our weaknesses. It we should fall, as we may, from time to time, it is this banner - our education, which must never be allowed to touch the ground. We should never forget that education is our first reason for existence as a university. Students, in particular, should always keep this in mind.

One of the singularly significant developments over the last couple of months has been the recently held national education conference at which a broad range of national, political, educational and community organisations participated. This conference agreed on a set of guiding principles for the future education system, including the right of all people - adults and children - to education and a corresponding obligation on the state to provide education and training. Clearly, the provision of education and training shall be linked to the development of human resources within national development aimed at the restructuring of the economy, redistribution, and the democratisation of society.

We would also have to place special emphasis on the redress of educational inequalities among historically disadvantaged sectors of society, particularly the youth, the disabled, adults, women, the unemployed, rural communities and black people in general.

Education should be based upon the principles of co-operation, critical thinking, and civic responsibility, and shall empower individuals for participation in all aspects of society. As we prepare for a democratic south, education will remain a central concern for us. It is therefore essential that we recognise this centrality and develop both short and long term objectives to realise this goal. In the short term we need to ensure that the immediate consequences of apartheid education are urgently addressed.

These include:
The reallocation of educational resources on a national basis according to national needs. Ensuring access to schooling,

particularly in the townships and rural areas. Improving the survival chances of our children in both primary and secondary schools in mathematics and sciences.

In this period of change, the minority government needs to cease all unilateral restructuring of education. In particular, its shortsighted moves to hand over national resources in the form of schools to the white community through its Model C policy, not only creates greater inequalities but entrenches the privileges of the white community.

Our majority objective in education is to develop a non-racial, non-sexist and democratic educational system. The realisation of this objective will not only ensure the development of an economically just society. Educational institutions such as universities and colleges have a major role to play in this task. The University of the North stands poised to play a significant role in this process. It is my belief that this university will respond to this challenge.

In conclusion I wish to thank you most profoundly, for the singular honour you deemed fit to bestow upon me, through my appointment as your chancellor. At all times I shall ensure that your trust in me is fully vindicated. Let us get down to work and make this university one of the brightest stars in this country.
Thank you.

Chapter 2:

University of the North: A detailed look

The University of the North (popularly known as Trufloop and as the University of Limpopo) has always been unashamedly Black and unapologetically Afro-centric in its curricula and research, seeking solutions for Africa and its indigenous people. The University's roots in the Black African experience and tradition are deep, lasting and permanent. It is a university of African people, and it has remained, *true to the native land,* the mother continent, the cradle of civilization. God has superintended its existence through the days it was created to serve apartheid by apartheid government -- the days of segregation, and the long night of racism and neglect by the apartheid government. From its establishment in 1959 the University of the North strove forcefully to present a true African image, not the image of Africa as seen through the eyes of Westernized Africans.

The University's vision and mission reflect its orientation towards Africa and its indigenous people.

For the very beginning, Turfloop, turned the apartheid government on its head. The University was created by the apartheid government to keep the African black people ignorant by placing them in on concentration campus away from city life and hypnotizing them into believing they were better than their fellow black brothers and sisters. The University, however, became an instrument for the abolition of the apartheid government and for the creation of an African State in South Africa.

The university enables students to teach themselves; this is the most valuable lesson. The mass meetings organized by the Student Representative Council were not just to discuss problems at the university. These meetings became a forum for public discourse on the clash of theoretical divergences and multidimensional ideological orientation of students. These discussions stimulated intellectual debate and social and political analysis. This kind of outside curriculum shaped students' ideological orientation and made them theoretically and practically aware of the circumstances in the country. Students acquired the ability to:

- think independently, rationally, and creatively
- improve their consciousness, intelligence, thinking - skills, discipline
- speak in public
- conduct research
- be innovative
- use common sense to solve problems
- develop and improve proficiency in their areas of interest

According to Jeffrey Pfeffer of Stanford University, students who attend a conventional university, as little as

5% percent of their curriculum will be relevant to success in a career. In other words, 95% of the curriculum is irrelevant. As Albert Einstein described his education:

> One had to cram all this stuff into one's mind, whether one liked it or not. This coercion had such a deterring effect that, after I had passed the final examination, I found the consideration of any scientific problems distasteful to me for an entire year... It is in fact nothing short of a miracle that the modern methods of instruction have not yet entirely strangled the holy curiosity of inquiry; for this delicate little plant, aside from stimulation, stands mainly in need of freedom; without this it goes to wrack and ruin without fail. It is a very grave mistake to think that the enjoyment of seeing and searching can be promoted by means of coercion and a sense of duty.

Thus instead of producing conformists to apartheid the University produced independent and self-reliant people.

An ideal society has a valid intellectual culture. The university is valuable to society to the extent that it enables an intellectual culture. A culture of university-trained intellectuals differs from one of workers. A complex society demands rational people who can use their minds to meet the demands of their society. The university that eschews intellectual cultivation in favor of professional training merely creates a class of individuals who have been degraded as rational beings, [Newman, p. 183], preventing them from performing their duty in a society that requires, deserves, and demands rational beings.

The consequences of the university shirking its responsibility to cultivate the intellect of its students are perilous. Writing in 1934, the Spanish philosopher Ortega y Gasset claimed that European culture predisposed its members to eschew reasoning altogether.

Modern universities are often praised for their scholarship or research but often these universities lack any sense of what they are doing.

The modern university has its origin in the monasteries of the Middle Ages. University lecturers belonged to a tradition in which excitement was to be found in books and in discoveries to which the rest of the world was indifferent, if not scornful. The university was only concerned with honing the skills of clerks who worked for the expanding government bureaucracy and the church.

Thus the student generalia of the Middle Ages survived the decay of Rome. Developed out of a profound reverence for an inherited culture, and from a disinherited, which is to say a no-instrumental passion for the truth.

On the eve of the Second World War, universities were treated as instruments for the promotion of economic prosperity.

Socrates is one of the greatest philosophers in history. He was accused of having neglected his own affairs, spending his time discussing virtue, justice and piety with his fellow

Athenians. Socrates as the harbinger of a university we immediately see that by entering the university realms entails sacrifice for the grand aim of assisting and improving the spiritual, moral and intellectual affairs of the greater society for the sake of it without being motivated by any personal rewards.

Like Socrates, the students of the University of the North were accused of neglecting their studies in order to criticize apartheid.

Socrates equated virtue with the knowledge of one's true self, holding that no one knowingly does wrong. He looked upon the soul as the seat of both waking consciousness and moral character. The ideals of black consciousness would shake the foundation of the university. It first publicly started with a final year student Abraham Ramothibe Onkgopotse Tiro speaking on behalf of the students during the University's Graduation Ceremony attacking what he saw as the extension of traditional white values at a university which was supposed to be black – he attacked especially the condescending values and attitudes of the University's white administrators.

Black consciousness is in essence the realization by the black person of the need to rally together with his fellow black people around the cause of their oppression – the blackness of their skin – and to operate as a group in order to rid themselves of the shackles that bind them to perpetual servitude. Black consciousness seeks to demonstrate the lie that being black is an aberration from the *normal,* which is being white. It is a manifestation of a new realization that by seeking to runaway from themselves and to emulate in values and traditions the white man, blacks are insulting the intelligence of whoever created them black.

Black consciousness in its centrality seeks to infuse the black community with a pride and vigor. The relationship between consciousness and emancipation is of paramount importance. Blacks no longer seek to reform the white system because it reform implies acceptance. The University of the North was created and run by whites for blacks.

To students like Tiro who imbibed the ideals of Black Consciousness, the University was an abomination. On Tiro's graduation day in 1972, he castigated Bantu education. Tiro's speech became known as the Turfloop Testimony. The impact of the speech was to be devastating not only for the University, but beyond cutting across villages and black townships influencing all universities (black and white alike).

Tiro was killed by the apartheid government because it claimed that he was corrupting Black people with his ideas about Black consciousness.

Universities before the Middle Ages were based on the pursuit of truth. Universities are judged by the size of their endowment and their research activities. Modern universities emphasize practical research to solve practical problems.

Kenneth Minogue asks why a modern university is primarily concerned with making people economically enterprising. He laments the fact that most graduates of the modern university graduate are looking for "jobs." Most of these graduates are homogenized creatures with the same tastes and opinions.

Minogue's views are supported by Ayn Rand's *The New Left.* One chapter is called "The Comprachicos" [the child-buyers]. The Comprachicos were notorious in seventeenth-century Spain for buying children, deforming them, and then displaying them as carnival attractions. Rand compares these children to students: *the student development was arrested, their minds are set to respond to slogans, as animals respond to a trainer's whistle, their brains are embalmed in the syrup of altruism as an automatic substitute for self-esteem… they would obey anyone, they need a master, they need to be told what to do. They are ready now to be used as cannon fodder – to attack, to bomb, to burn, to murder, to fight in the streets and die in the gutters. They are a trained pack of miserably impotent freaks, ready to be unleashed against anyone.*

A modern university reflecting Socratic ideals is the developmental university similar to University for Development in Ghana, West Africa.

The university's mission is to identify itself with the realities of the predominantly rural communities in northern Ghana. The university was created to effect a paradigm shift in higher education, in order to solve the country's entrenched socioeconomic problems. In keeping with its innovative approach to higher learning, it has established campuses across the northern region, and in its operational area of Brong Ahafo. As a result of its success, the institution is now under enormous pressure, particularly from rural communities, to continue its civic engagement.

On the global platform there has been an attempt to reshape the modern concept of the university to restore it to its original ideals. Sister Joan Delaney wrote an article describing reform initiatives. We share some of these initiatives here.

The terms being bandied around to replace the modern term of a university are Multiversity, anti-university, open university, critical university. These terms are attempts to define the function of the modern university or to explain what it is missing. Multiuniversity is the term most often used by presidents of large colleges and universities in the United States.

The term "anti-university" connotes dissatisfaction with the curriculum and degree requirements of the modern university. The terms open, or critical, university are used interchangeably.

An open entry policy does not consider applicants' academic achievements for entry to most undergraduate and postgraduate courses. An example of an open university is Rushmore University. According to the Rushmore University website:

In 1996, we challenged the modern day university educational establishment. We have adapted the 500-year-old Oxford Tutorial Method to the modern capabilities of the Internet to provide our students with the academic freedom to control how, where, when and what they learn. Our programs are based on written papers. You tailor your own curriculum with the guidance of our renowned Professors. There are no exams or required courses.

Founded in 1096 in Oxford, England, Oxford University is the oldest English-speaking university in the world. Over the nine centuries since then, Oxford has graduated five kings, 40 Nobel Prize winners, 25 British Prime Ministers, nine current holders of the Order of Merit, three Saints, 18 Cardinals and 85 Archbishops.

The Tutorial Method has been used at Oxford for more than 500 years. It is a rigorous, individualized method of teaching and learning. Each Oxford student has an academic tutor (an Advisor or Professor). An Oxford education emphasizes learning to think through research and writing. Oxford students are responsible for planning their own time and ensuring that the requisite work is accomplished.

Oxford has characteristics not usually seen at American universities, among them:
- Students are treated as individuals.
- It is easy to meet with faculty members, even senior ones.
- Independent learning is emphasized as opposed to teaching by the faculty.
- Learning is accomplished through research and writing.
- Students are expected to discuss their written work with their tutors one-on-one.
- Degree programs are more specialized.

In contrast, most American universities offer their programs and courses with:

- Large lecture classes
- Standardized courses
- Negligible writing assignments
- Little one-on-one contact with faculty
- Little customization of an individual student's program
- Negligible attention to the individual student

At Rushmore, we have adapted the Oxford Tutorial Method to the online environment of the Internet and email. You communicate with your Professor by email or telephone as often as you need to. If you happen to live near a Faculty member, you may arrange to meet with him or her in person. This personal approach to learning, featuring frequent interaction with your Professor, affords the Rushmore student greater flexibility and support than at conventional schools.

Oxford students must be able to present and defend their own opinions and to accept constructive criticism and advice. Tackling topics in depth and defending the arguments in their written work sharpens their thinking. As a student at Rushmore, you will have the benefit of the Oxford Tutorial Method. Our online adaptation of the Oxford approach will help you to develop such skills as:

- Time management: the ability to organize your own work schedule rather than have it imposed on you
- Argumentation: the ability to present a point of view
- Critical assessment: the ability to understand, evaluate and respond to the ideas of others

As with the Oxford student, your success with the tutorial approach depends upon your ability to study independently under the guidance of your Professor. The primary purpose of the Oxford Tutorial Method is to teach you how to teach yourself. This is the most important academic lesson you will ever learn.

Chapter 3:

Ideological Underpinnings

What ideological orientations informed university students' outlook? Above all, the students were opposed to Bantu education. Act of 1953. This dates to the early 1970s when the president of the SRC, Abraham Onkgopotse Tiro delivered a speech that denounced the Bantu Education Act of 1953; this became known as the 'Turfloop Testimony'. Because of his speech, Tiro was expelled from the University.

Subsequently he was offered a post as a history teacher by Legau Mathabathe, the Headmaster of the Morris Isaacson High School in Soweto, where he shared with the students some of the ideas in the Turfloop Testimony and started a campaign to encourage students to question the validity and content of the history books prescribed by the Department of Bantu Education. (source)

So Tiro brought the Turfloop Testimony from the University to Soweto. The Testimony was instrumental in the formation of South African Student Movement (SASM). SASM led the famous 1976 Soweto Uprisings.

According to Assata Shakur's website:

The eruption of student uprisings in June 1976 has to be seen in its proper perspective. Today, organisations and individuals have claimed responsibility for the uprising. However, events prior to June 16, 1976 will show that no one other than the students themselves, under the leadership of the SASM (of which Abraham Tiro was the principal architect), can claim responsibility.

Before to June 1976, there was no enough pressure exerted on the South African regime militarily either because the organisations lacked the capacity or the political will to do so.

In fact the speech by Onkgopotse Tiro was preceded by a series of boycotts starting in 1970. In 1970 the SRC organized a boycott protesting against the inferior status accorded the black man in his so called institution. Precisely they resented the paternalistic attitude of the white government as reflected in the composition of the university council. These were followed by a boycott of the investiture of the chancellor, and took the opportunity to focus attention on the paradoxical nature of the university. It was their contention that if the university belonged to blacks, it had to bear the stamp of black authority; and further, that if the university was meant to reflect and enhance the black experience, the range of courses offered should, wherever possible, contain a large component of black perspective.

It was also at this time that black students from all universities found themselves galvanized and formed the South African Students' Organisation (SASO). Its membership was exclusively black. The reasoning for the exclusive black membership of the organization was that you are *either part of the solution or part of the problem.* It was further reasoned that whites students cannot be accepted because they have defined themselves all the years as *part of the problem* because of their attitude of political supremacy.

One important thing which worked in favor of the newly formed SASO was that it received the blessings of the governing councils on all black campuses because the white vice chancellors of these black campuses saw in SASO the manifestation of the ideology of apartheid or separate development, particularly that black students were always a problem within the multi-racial National Union of South African Students (NUSAS). NUSAS was abandoned by black students because it was considered by black students as an ineffective forum to express their experiences and fulfill their aspirations. It was argued that NUSAS essentially an English language university affair, was liberal and patronizing to black students.

The birth of SASO at the University of the North opened a way for the black faculty to assert themselves in the same fashion. Since the establishment of the University in 1960, black and white faculty belonged to the same staff association. But in 1971 there was a growing feeling amongst the black staff that because of the differential treatment that they received, that they could bargain more effectively in a separate staff association. In 1972, black faculty applied for recognition by Council. The result was the formation of the Black Academic Staff

Association (BASA). Formal recognition of BASA was received in 1973.

Tiro made his historic speech at the Graduation Ceremony at the University of the North in 1972 which focused attention on the paradoxical nature of the University in which power and authority resided in the white hands, the blacks occupying advisory and token positions. Let us look at the reaction of the University administration to Tiro's speech:

As we noted Tiro was expelled. The reason given for the expulsion was that Tiro had chosen a wrong occasion to give such a speech he gave, and so embarrassed the University in the presence of its friends at the graduation ceremony.

Protesting the expulsion of Tiro as a flagrant violation of freedom of speech, students at the university *walked out*. This revolution spread to other black universities. A revolution is like an avalanche; it is hard to stop.

Tiro became a hero to a whole generation of high school students, and by the end of 1972, the popularity of the SASO was at its peak. In 1972, SASO's newsletter had 4,000 readers.

After Tiro had delivered his speech the Council of the University of the North panicked, and held an emergency meeting in Pretoria on 15 May 1972. The Council resolved that a Committee of Inquiry be appointed from its own members, but with two members of the exclusively black Advisory Council. The purpose of the Committee of

Inquiry was to investigate the causes of student unrest at the University and at the University of Fort Hare.

The Committee's terms of reference were:

....to investigate the underlying fundamental causes of student unrest at the University of the North and to report on the steps necessary to be taken in the future to avoid situations of a similar nature...

The Committee stated:

> The fundamental cause of student unrest is of a political nature. The other causes that the Committee found are of lesser importance. Student politics and views are entirely unrealistic. They are influenced by outside bodies, thoughts and philosophies and their parents themselves, in exploiting real or imaginary grievances arising from the South African political situation. Students who have political aspirations should not seek to use the campus as a platform for the expression of thoughts on matters that are in any case out of bounds of their activities. The political situation and the future role of the students in his own Homeland should be conveyed to students by the lecturing staff, especially the black staff. The students are preparing themselves for a career with the assistance of the South African Government. Everything must therefore be done to achieve this aim. This matter must be given deep thought by all who are concerned with the education of the black student.

The Committee of Inquiry then began its investigative work, and found that black awareness or consciousness was to be found in theology, theatre and cinema, sociology, history and in all spheres of black experience. It further discovered that in terms of black awareness *everything must have relevance to the black community*. The Committee therefore came to the realization that *this awareness is supported and assisted by many*.

Consequently the Committee recommended that:

> Note must be taken of this movement of black awareness or consciousness which at this stage does not seem to be adequately organized due to lack of leaders. This black awareness or consciousness will increase and if understood could be guided into channels to the advantage of everybody in South Africa.

Its findings on the South African Students' Organisation (SASO) however were noteworthy:

> The South African Students' Organisation (SASO) has the support of the black community. Nothing could therefore be achieved by banning this organisation from the campus. An attempt must be made to sublimate its efforts of students' activity.

The Committee noted that on one hand, that black students must be taught to accept the Homelands, which are based on ethnicity and tribes, and that black awareness or consciousness be promoted.

The Black Consciousness movement was heightened in the University in 1974, when Frelimo became the provisional government in Mozambique on 25 September, marking the end of a bloody revolution and four hundred years of Portuguese rule. The students transplanted the Mozambique spirit into the University Campus by organizing a rally on the same day. The triumph in Mozambique by black people propelled and moved the conviction of students to the peak affirming in political terms, of the Black Consciousness and the reinforced black identity amongst students in the continent of their birth.

Thus the paradox of the University of the North continued, here was a university established to destroy the minds of black people. Here was a University established to educate black people to be obedient to the apartheid racist government. Here was the University of the North, itself a function of the apartheid racist government policy. Here were black students in an ethnic university asserting over-riding black values which were incompatible with the ethos of the policy apartheid and subjugation.

The tension between the South African government and the students reached a boiling point. The rally that was organized by the University of the North students was undertaken despite the nationwide ban on pro-Frelimo rallies. Heavily armed police officers were called to the campus, where they scuffled with students.

On 1 November 1974, the State President appointed a one-man judicial Commission of Inquiry called Snyman Commission after Mr. Justice J.H. Snyman.

The Commission was to inquire into and report on:

1. The events of 25 September 1974 on the campus of the University of the North with the view to determining the causes that gave rise thereto and the part played therein by the University Management, the Students Representative Council and any other organization of either the students or the lecturers, with specific attention to:-
   (a) the relationship on the campus between the black and the white academic staff and the students; and
   (b) related matters concerning the present and future management of the University of the North, including possible interference therein by the Black Academic Staff Association;
2. To make recommendations in the view of the findings, which the Commission deems necessary.

The Commission concluded that

- The pro-Frelimo rally was just a symptom of a vast and complex malady, and that the University of the North was *ensnared in a much broader and deeper problem than just a university situation, namely the situation between white and black outside the University.*

- There is much anti-white sentiment amongst students and black staff, and suggested that the underlying causes had to be examined "in the light of the ideology of Black Consciousness which has taken roots among the nations of the world in the past few decades.

- The black students of the University of the North reject the University because they see it as a product of apartheid.

The suggestions of the Commission were startling. The Commission suggested that …

- this Black consciousness is aggravated in the black community by statutory and traditional restrictions which have been imposed on the blacks mainly in the interests of the whites, and the often unpleasant personal experiences of blacks, especially the urbanized, westernized and sophisticated blacks, have had encounters with many whites in the streets, in shops and in other public places, which impair their human dignity.

- It is especially the humiliating behavior of whites outside campus towards the blacks of the University of the North which has repercussions on the campus and frustrates the well-meaning attempts of the [white] University authorities and the white staff in general to create healthy relations on the campus, and furthermore gives rise to an abhorrence of the policy of separate development [apartheid] in the blacks.

The Commission examined the need for a black take-over of the University. It considered such a move of vital importance because blacks attending the University of the

North thought that whites continually took decisions for or on their behalf without giving blacks any meaningful say in them. This tended to deprive them of their dignity and alienate them from the institution meant to serve their communities.

The Commission acknowledged that:

- As long as the University is not accepted by its people as its own it cannot play a fruitful role in the community. That is why the takeover of the management of the University by blacks should not be deterred longer than necessary.

Chapter 4:

The Turfloop Testimony

Let us return to the speech which Abraham Onkgopotse Tiro made in 1972.

Tiro started by quoting Prime Minister Vorster's statement to the effect that no Black man had landed in trouble for fighting for what was legally his. He then criticized the white administration of the University and its discrimination against blacks. He was critical of the fact that at a Black university, the bookshop was run by whites, and that a contract to supply meat to the University was given to a white person. In his view it was wrong for white students to be given all of the vacation jobs at the University, and that there was not enough room in the Hall to accommodate all Black parents who had come to watch their children graduate. He then commented on the debate between integration and separation, and ended with an appeal for Black unity.

Tiro's speech was not deeply revolutionary; proposing a debate on race and the problems faced by black people was accepted practice, and yet his speech's gesture reached all universities in South Africa. From then on battle lines between blacks and whites were drawn at all universities.

Tiro's speech embarrassed the white administration. Some black faculty members tried to persuade Tiro to apologize and retract the speech. Tiro, being a man of principle, refused and told them that he had only spoken the truth.

A few weeks after the speech. the Vice Chancellor issued a circular to all university staff indicating that the University Council had expelled all students. However all students that were expelled from the University had the opportunity to re-apply for admission. Tiro's re-application was turned down.

Here is the full text speech of Onkgopotse Abram Ramothibi Tiro the then President of the SRC of the University of the North. The speech was delivered at the University Graduation Ceremony on 29 April 1972. Tiro had been elected by the students to deliver the address on their behalf during the graduation ceremony.

Mass protests by the student body followed news of Tiro's expulsion. The entire student body was then expelled. Protests erupted at both black and white universities and government reaction then followed. Mr. Tiro eventually fled to Botswana. In 1974 Mr. Tiro was killed by a parcel bomb explosion sent to him by the South African police.

Graduation Speech by Onkgopotse Tiro at the University of the North, 29 April 1972

Mr. Chancellor, Mr. Vice Chancellor and gentlemen, allow me to start off by borrowing language from our Prime Minister, Mr. Vorster. In June last year, Mr. Vorster said, "No Black man has landed in trouble for fighting for what is legally his." Although I don't know how far true this is, I make this statement my launch pad.

R. D Briensmead, an American lay preacher says, *He who withholds the truth or debars men from motives of its expediency, is either a coward, a criminal or both.* Therefore Mr. Chancellor I will try as much as possible to say nothing else but the truth. And to me *truth* means *practical reality.* Addressing us on the occasion of the formal opening of this university Mr. [Cedric] Phatudi, a Lebowa territorial authority officer, said that in as much as there is American Education, there had to be **Bantu Education.** Ladies and gentlemen, I am conscientiously bound to differ with him. In America there is nothing like Negro Education, Red Indian Education, and White American Education. They have American Education common to all Americans. But in South Africa, we have Bantu Education, Indian Education, Coloured Education and European Education. We do not have a system of education common to all South Africans. What is there in European Education which is not good for the African? We want a system of education which is common to all South Africans.

In theory Bantu Education gives our parents a say in our education but in practice the opposite is true. At this University, U. E D [University Education Diploma] students are forced to study Philosophy of Education through the medium of Afrikaans. When we want to know why, we are told that the senate has decided so. Apparently this senate is our parents. Time and again I ask myself: How do Black lecturers contribute to the administration of this University? For if you look at all the committees, they are predominantly White if not completely White. Here and there one finds two or three Africans who, in the opinion of students are White Black men. We have a Students' Dean without duties. We feel that if it is in any way necessary to have Students' Dean, we must elect our own Dean. We know people who can represent us.

The Advisory Council is said to be representing our parents. How can it represent them when they have not elected it? These people must of necessity please the man who appointed them. This Council consists of Chiefs who have never been to University. How can they know the needs of students when they have not subjected to the same conditions. Those who have not been to University have never studied Bantu Education. What authentic opinion can they express when they don't know how painful it is to study under a repugnant system of education? I wonder if this Advisory knows that a Black man has been most unceremoniously kicked out of the bookshop. Apparently, this is reserved for Whites. According Council to the policy of separate development [apartheid], Van Schaiks has no right to run a bookshop here. A White member of the Administration has been given the meat contract to supply the University – a Black University. Those who amorphously support the policy may say that there are no Black people to supply it. My answer to them is: why are they not able to supply the University? What is the cause? Is it not conveniently done that they are not in a position to supply these commodities?

White students are given vacation jobs at this university when there are students who could not get their results due to outstanding fees. Why does the Administration not give these jobs to these students? These White students have 11 universities where they can get vacation jobs. Does the Administration expect me to get a vacation job at the University of Pretoria? Right now, our parents have come all the way from their homes only to be locked outside. We are told that the hall is full. I do not accept the argument that there is no accommodation for them. In 1970, when the Administration wanted to accommodate everybody, a tent was put up and close-circuit television was installed.

Front seats are given to people who cannot even cheer us. My father is seated there at the back. My dear people, shall we ever get a fair deal in this land? The land of our fathers. The system is failing. It is failing because even those recommended it strongly, as the only solution to racial problems in South Africa, fail to adhere to the letter and the spirit of the policy. According to the policy we expected Dr. Eiselen to decline Chancellorship in favour of a Black man. My dear parents, these are injustices no normal student can tolerate-no matter who he is and where he comes from.

In the light of what has been said above, the challenge to every Black graduate in this country lies in the fact that the guilt of all wrongful actions in South Africa, restriction without trial, repugnant legislation, expulsions from schools, rests on all those who do not actively dissociate themselves from and work for the eradication of the system breeding such evils.

To those who wholeheartedly support the policy of apartheid I say: Do you think that the White minority can willingly commit political suicide by creating numerous states which might turn out to be hostile in the future? We Black graduates, by virtue of our age and academic standing are being called upon to bear greater responsibilities in the liberation of our people. Our so-called leaders have become the bolts of the same machine which is crushing us as a nation. We have to go back to them and educate them. Times are changing and we should change with them. The magic story of human achievement gives irrefutable proof that as soon as nationalism is awakened among the intelligentsia, it becomes the vanguard in the struggle against alien rule. Of what use will be your education if is not linked with the entire continent of Africa it is meaningless. Remember that Mrs. Suzman said, *There is one thing which the minister cannot do: He cannot ban ideas from men's minds.*

In conclusion Mr. Chancellor I say: Let the Lord be praised, for the day shall come, when all shall be free to breathe the air of freedom which is theirs to breathe and when the day shall have come, no man, no matter how many tanks he has, will reverse the course of events.

God Bless you all.

Chapter 5:

Soweto Uprising

Tiro continued to share his Turfloop testimony ideals with the students at the high school at which he taught after his expulsion. His ideals and his South African Student Movement (SASM) unified with the others launched a series of events that culminated in the June 16, 1976 uprising.

In this chapter we focus on the conditions of Morris Isaacson High School when Tiro was teaching there. In order to do this we quote here the testimony of his colleague Fanyana Mazibuko before the government's Truth and Reconciliation Committee (TRC). Anyone who felt that he or she was a victim of its violence was invited to come forward and be heard. Perpetrators of violence could also give testimony and request amnesty from prosecution.

Fanyana Mazibuko's Testimony before the TRC:

> Morris Isaacson was a highly disciplined school, almost military in its discipline. The other side of Morris Isaacson is that it was politically aware.

In my arrival at Morris Isaacson a number of things happened which indicated this. Examples of this political awareness and the leadership of the principal as a politically aware person is firstly the Tiro case. In the Tiro case the principal decided to employ a person who had been expelled from a university, against the wishes of the Department of Education. And secondly there was the allowing by the principal of the formation of several organisations on the premises, including for example the formation of the organisation which was first called the Azanian People's Writers Association, which was initially AZAPOA, but later changed to Medupi Writer's Association. And also the principal was not easily compliant with instructions from the Department, example, when we were instructed to teach in Afrikaans he invited the Inspector who was giving this instruction, and he told him it will not be done.

On the morning of June 16, now I will be very brief on June 16 because a lot of things have already been said, at the school assembly in the morning we went through the normal procedure, at the end of the praying a certain student by the name of Tsietsi Mashinini climbed onto the platform and he started a song and placards went up and he led the students out of the school. Because we expected there was going to be a march we simply stood aside and we were in agreement with this.

An account of the multiplier effects of the uprising is available at the Michigan University: Overcoming Apartheid

Soweto Student Uprising

As the mid-year exams approached, boycotts took place in many Soweto schools (Ndlovu). It was around that time that the older students of the South African Students Movement (SASM) decided to organize a mass protest in Soweto. In a 1977 interview, Tebello Motapanyane, then secretary general of SASM, provided an account of the action committee's decision to launch the protest:

We took a decision to inform the staff that we totally reject the half-yearly examinations and were not going to write the exams until our demands were met. The Naledi branch called a meeting under SASM on Sunday, June 13 where it was actually decided that there should be positive action from all the high schools and secondary schools in Soweto. We discussed Afrikaans and how to make the government aware that we opposed their decision. The delegates decided that there should be a mass demonstration from the Soweto students as a whole.

The brutal killing of the school children on June 16, 1976, shocked the international community. Newspapers across the world published Sam Nzima's photograph of a dying Hector Peterson on their front page. In the meantime, South African security forces, equipped with armored tanks and live ammunition, poured into Soweto. Their instructions were to shoot to kill, for the sake of *law and order.* By nightfall another eleven more people had been shot dead (Bonner). Students in Soweto responded by pelting the police with stones and attacking what they regarded to be symbols of the apartheid government. Across much of Soweto government buildings and liquor stores were looted and burned.

On the second day of the uprising, the violence spread to African townships in the West Rand and Johannesburg. At the University of Witwatersrand, police broke up a group of 400 white students who had been marching to express their solidarity with the pupils of Soweto. On the third day, police began placing youth protestors in jail; students later testified to being tortured while imprisoned.

What began as a local demonstration against the Afrikaans language decree quickly turned into a countrywide youth uprising against apartheid oppression. Kgati Sathekge, current Director for Communications and Marketing for the Ministry of Social Development, was one of thousands of students from Atterridgeville, an African township near Pretoria, who took part in the protests in that region.

In his 2006 interview, he explained: We could not accept that type of behavior . . . personally it was a great shock. We started organizing protests . . . On June 21 when students came to school we mobilized them and said we're not going to go to school that day, we'll engage in protest marches throughout the township . . . Different government offices were targeted and burned down including . . . buildings seen as symbols of oppression [such as] government stores, bottle (alcohol) stores, beer halls.

The police shootings and the defiant response of African students in Soweto emboldened youth throughout the country to wage protests. Students in Port Elizabeth mobilized in their schools, leading to a conflict between the police and a crowd of 4,000 high school students and township residents en route to the local soccer stadium that left eight residents dead. Shepi Mati, who arrived in Port Elizabeth at the end of 1976 to attend high school, recalls the violence and tension of that time: On any given day, you would just hear this sound – it was a very ominous sound – you could feel it in the air. And suddenly there would be a Caspir that comes past, a police armored car – woosh – throwing tear gas or shooting as it goes past. This was really my welcome to Port Elizabeth

About 5 000 students across all Soweto participated. Police during that day killed almost 700 students.

These country wide unrests as sparked by the Tiro's Turfloop Testimony finally reached the African National Congress (ANC) Headquarters in Lusaka Zambia. The ANC this time was banned from operating in the country by the South African government. It was operating in the neighboring countries with the headquarters in Lusaka, Zambia. Its imminent leader Nelson Mandela was arrested and banished to Robben Island Prison.

The ANC relayed the countrywide unrests to Nelson Mandela in Robben Island prison. After hearing about the events Mandela wrote this letter addressed to Soweto community.

'UNITE! MOBILISE! FIGHT ON! BETWEEN THE ANVIL OF UNITED MASS ACTION AND THE HAMMER OF THE ARMED STRUGGLE WE SHALL CRUSH APARTHEID!'
This message was Mandela's call after the Soweto uprising of 1976. with an introduction by O R Tambo, President of the banned ANC operating in Lusaka, Zambia;

The African National Congress brings you this URGENT CALL TO UNITY AND MASS ACTION by political prisoners on Robben Island to all patriots of our motherland. Nelson Mandela and hundreds of our comrades have been in the racist regime's prisons for more than 17 years. This message by Nelson Mandela addressed to the struggling masses of our country was written to deal with the present crisis gripping our enemy and in the aftermath of the Soweto uprisings. It was smuggled out of Robben Island prison under very difficult conditions and has taken over two years to reach us. None the less we believe the message remains fresh and valid and should be presented to our people. His call to unity and mass action is of particular importance in this Year of the Charter - 25th anniversary of the Freedom Charter. The ANC urges you to respond to this call and make 1980 a year of united mass struggle.

Oliver Tambo: President, ANC

MANDELA'S CALL

RACISTS RULE BY THE GUN!

The gun has played an important part in our history. The resistance of the black man to white colonial intrusion was crushed by the gun. Our struggle to liberate ourselves from white domination is held in check by force of arms. From conquest to the present the story is the same. Successive white regimes have repeatedly massacred unarmed defenceless blacks. And wherever and whenever they have pulled out their guns the ferocity of their fire has been trained on the African people.

Apartheid is the embodiment of the racialism, repression and inhumanity of all previous white supremacist regimes. To see the real face of apartheid we must look beneath the veil of constitutional formulas, deceptive phrases and playing with words.

The rattle of gunfire and the rumbling of Hippo armoured vehicles since June 1976 have once again torn aside that veil. Spread across the face of our country, in black townships, the racist army and police have been pouring a hail of bullets killing and maiming hundreds of black men, women and children. The toll of the dead and injured already surpasses that of all past massacres carried out by this regime.

Apartheid is the rule of the gun and the hangman. The Hippo, the FN rifle and the gallows are its true symbols. These remain the easiest resort, the ever ready solution of the race-mad rulers of South Africa.

VAGUE PROMISES, GREATER REPRESSION . . .

In the midst of the present crisis, while our people count the dead and nurse the injured, they ask themselves: what lies ahead?

From our rulers we can expect nothing. They are the ones who give orders to the soldier crouching over his rifle: theirs is the spirit that moves the finger that caresses the trigger.

Vague promises, tinkerings with the machinery of apartheid, constitution juggling, massive arrests and detentions side by side with renewed overtures aimed at weakening and forestalling the unity of us blacks and dividing the forces of change - these are the fixed paths along which they will move. For they are neither capable nor willing to heed the verdict of the masses of our people.

THE VERDICT OF JUNE 16!

That verdict is loud and clear: apartheid has failed. Our people remain unequivocal in its rejection. The young and the old, parent and child, all reject it. At the forefront of this 1976/77 wave of unrest were our students and youth. They come from the universities, high schools and even primary schools. They are a generation whose whole education has been under the diabolical design of the racists to poison the minds and brainwash our children into docile subjects of apartheid rule. But after more than twenty years of Bantu Education the circle is closed and nothing demonstrates the utter bankruptcy of apartheid as the revolt of our youth.

The evils, the cruelty and the inhumanity of apartheid have been there from its inception. And all blacks - Africans, Coloureds and Indians - have opposed it all along the line. What is now unmistakable, what the current wave of unrest has sharply highlighted, is this: that despite all the window-dressing and smooth talk, apartheid has become intolerable.

This awareness reaches over and beyond the particulars of our enslavement. The measure of this truth is the recognition by our people that under apartheid our lives, individually and collectively, count for nothing.

UNITE !

We face an enemy that is deep rooted; an enemy entrenched and determined not to yield. Our march to freedom is long and difficult. But both within and beyond our borders the prospects of victory grow bright.

The first condition for victory is black unity. Every effort to divide the blacks, to woo and pit one black group against another, must be vigorously repulsed. Our people - African, Coloured, Indian and democratic whites - must be united into a single massive and solid wall of resistance, of united mass action.

Our struggle is growing sharper. This is not the time for the luxury of division and disunity. At all levels and in every walk of life we must close ranks. Within the ranks of the people differences must be submerged to the achievement of a single goal - the complete overthrow of apartheid and racist domination.

VICTORY IS CERTAIN !

The revulsion of the world against apartheid is growing and the frontiers of white supremacy are shrinking. Mozambique and Angola are free and the war of liberation gathers force in Namibia and Zimbabwe. The soil of our country is destined to be the scene of the fiercest fight and the sharpest battles to rid our continent of the last vestiges of white minority rule.

The world is on our side. The OAU, the UN and the anti-apartheid movement continue to put pressure on the racist rulers of our country. Every effort to isolate South Africa adds strength to our struggle.

At all levels of our struggle, within and outside the country, much has been achieved and much remains to be done. But victory is certain!

WE SALUTE ALL OF YOU!

We who are confined within the grey walls of the Pretoria regime's prisons reach out to our people. With you we count those who have perished by means of the gun and the hangman's rope. We salute all of you - the living, the injured and the dead. For you have dared to rise up against the tyrant's might.

Even as we bow at their graves we remember this: the dead live on as martyrs in our hearts and minds, a reproach to our disunity and the host of shortcomings that accompany divisions among the oppressed, a spur to our efforts to close ranks, and a reminder that the freedom of our people is yet to be won.

We face the future with confidence. For the guns that serve apartheid cannot render it unconquerable. Those who live by the gun shall perish by the gun.

UNITE! MOBILISE! FIGHT ON!

Between the anvil of united mass action and the hammer of the armed struggle we shall crush apartheid and white minority racist rule.

AMANDLA NGAWETHU! MATLA KE A RONA!

The Death of Onkgopotse Tiro

As we noted earlier Tiro fled South Africa into Botswana to escape from the police. In Botswana he taught at a Catholic school.

Onkopotse Tiro was killed by a parcel bomb in February 1974 in Gaborone (the Capital City of Botswana). Patrick Tlhagoane – who is Onkgopotse Tiro's cousin, requested Eric Molobi to accompany him to Botswana to identify Tiro's body. They left the following day for Kgale Catholic Mission where Onkgopotse Tiro had been teaching. They were accompanied by Ben Tlhagoane.

Patrick Tlhagoane testifies that when they arrived there, they went to the house where Tiro had received the parcel bomb. The coal stove which had been in the middle of the room had been shattered by the impact of the bomb. Patrick Tlhagoane, Ben Tlagoane and Eric Molobi cleaned the room and washed Tiro's blood from the walls and the floor.

From there, they went to see Onkgopotse Tiro's body at St. Marina hospital in Gaborone. When they arrived, the nursing sister in charge asked them if they were sure that they wanted to see the deceased. To which they responded in the affirmative. She left for a few minutes and returned with some tablets for them to drink before they saw the remains of Tiro. Patrick Tlhagoane says that he clearly remembers Eric Molobi saying that; "We do not want the tablets. Let us feel the pain."

They then went to see the deceased. No one will ever be able to describe the pain that they felt at that moment.

They were brave. They went home and told the family that *ga a bonwe.* i.e. no one is allowed to see the corpse. The three of them were therefore the only close relatives that saw Tiro's body after it had been devastated by the bomb.

Two weeks before his death, Onkgopotse Tiro, as President of SASM, had sent a message to the 5th SASO General Students Council. In it he said: *from this meeting you will be called names … this is not new. Our forerunners have suffered all this. No struggle can come to an end without casualties. It is only through determination, absolute commitment and positive self-assertion that we shall overcome.*

Chapter 6:

The formation of United Democratic Front

The 1970s mass protests ushered in a new wave of revolution in the 1980s. the formation of the United Democratic Front (UDF) began in the early 1980s when at a conference in Johannesburg on 23 January 1983, Allan Boesak called for a united front of churches, civic associations, trade unions, student organizations, and sports bodies to fight oppression.

At the conference, the leaders of the Transvaal anti-SAIC Committee (TASC) proposed that a committee explore the feasibility of such a front. After heated discussions, TASC decided to join organizations in a regional and federal structure, as long as they were non-racist. The UDF had a Christian heritage, like the ANC, and resembled a faction of the ANC, but it distanced itself from the armed struggle.

The next step was to establish regional committees. In May the Natal UDF was launched, followed by the Transvaal in June and the Western Cape in July. A new Interim National Committee was formed with black and white members from each region. An important two-day planning meeting was held by the committee at the end of July in Johannesburg, attended by Albertina Sisulu, Mewa Ramgobin and Steve Tshwete. The committee discussed when to launch the UDF and, although they needed time to organize, decided on 20 August, when the government planned to introduce Tricameral legislation. This left the committee with only three weeks. They discussed principles and documents, and decided on a logo and slogan: *UDF Unites, Apartheid Divides.*

Groups working with government, with homeland state structures, and groups that broke sport and cultural boycotts were not be allowed to join UDF.

On 20 August 1983, the UDF was formed in a community hall in Rocklands, Mitchell's Plain in Cape Town. Frank Chikane, who had played an important role in the formation of the UDF, was the first speaker. Chikane described the day as being a turning point in the struggle for freedom. The keynote speaker, Allan Boesak, spoke of bringing together a range of groups and unity among those fighting for freedom. A list of tasks was drawn up, focusing on organization building and highlighting the aim of the UDF as an organization that represented all South Africans.

In the afternoon, the conference adjourned and the rally began. The doors were opened to allow in approximately 10,000 people. Loudspeakers and video-screens broadcasted the proceedings. Frances Baard opened the rally, and speeches focused on Charterism. What was significant about the day was the amount of support from

565 organizations. Four hundred of these were already regional affiliates of the UDF.

However, the formation was actually the result of social, economic and political changes that had been taking place since the Soweto Uprising. A new, more militant culture had emerged, that led to the formation of many civic, youth, student, worker, women and other organizations. There was also increased support for Charterism and mass organization. In the immediate post-Soweto period, study groups appeared in townships across the country. Some of these were very informal but others, such as one led by Joe Gqabi in Soweto, focused on Charterist and ANC principles. These groups spread ideas, recruited new members, and spread into other circles. Initially the study groups had little or no contact with each other. In the late 1970s there were some attempts to get groups to unite, and in 1979 Popo Molefe and Vincent Mogane launched AZAPO in Soweto, with Molefe calling for a front in Soweto to unite AZAPO, COSAS, trade unions and other organizations. This was unsuccessful, and although Molefe left AZAPO, he continued to call for united resistance in the early 1980s. At the same time, the ANC saw the need for a broad organization inside South Africa, united in its opposition to apartheid. These developments culminated in the formation of the UDF in 1983.

The backbone of UDF in the Northern Transvaal was the University of the North. In 1984 Peter Nchabeleng was among the first member and the regional chair of the Northern Transvaal. While serving in the UDF he was in charge of ANC network in Northern Transvaal.

Barely two months after his election as chairperson of the UDF Northern Transvaal he was detained and murdered by the Lebowa police. He was succeeded by the Vice Chairperson Louis Mnguni, a philosophy lecturer at the University of the North. Louis Mnguni was succeeded by Thabo Makunyane, who had been a friend of Abram Tiro.

The secretary of the regional executive was Joyce Mabudafhasi, a library assistant at the University of the North. Mabudafhasi was once detained during the 1976 uprising. She was later seriously injured when her house in Mankweng, the township adjacent to the University of the North, was firebombed.

The Publicity Secretary of the UDF Northern Transvaal was Peter Mokaba, a former student at the University of the North. Alfred Mabake Makaleng, a law student at the University of the North was regional organizer. However Alfred Mabake Makaleng was detained in June 1986 and died in prison two years later.

The UDF Northern Transvaal had meager facilities but it had access to the resources of the University of the North. The University of the North played a tremendous role as the centre of communication, coordination, ideological direction, and recruitment. If offered sanctuary to activists on the run from police.

On the national stage, the University of the North was the ANC headquarters from Lusaka, Zambia. Hence the University was nicknamed Lusaka.

Student leaders at the University had access to telephones, photocopy machines, meeting facilities, and occasionally cars. Sports outings to other black universities were used for "spreading the gospel."

The UDF and the ANC leadership in Lusaka, Zambia encouraged people to study at Turfloop rather than other universities because of Turfloop's central role in the fight against apartheid.

In 1983, students from Sekhukhuneland met at Turfloop to discuss the formation of organizations in their home villages. Over the holidays, students from Turfloop formed youth groups in their villages; when the University re-opened they would meet at the student centre to exchange experiences.

Networking with the villages was an important source of organizational know-how and political education.

They taught the youth in the villages how to conduct meetings and ran community workshops on Marxism-Leninism.

In spite of persistent police raids and closures of the University of the North students still organized freely on the campus. In 1986 the University management requested a full time patrol of the University by South African soldiers.

Chapter 7:

Black Academic Staff Association

The Black Academic Staff Association focused on the paradoxical nature of the University in which power and authority resided in white hands.

The Black Academic Staff Association maintained that it had the responsibility to give the University of the North and the country as a whole the benefit of its understanding of the problems of higher education for blacks in South Africa. For this reason, the Black Academic Staff Association submitted a detailed memorandum to the Commissioner in defense of the students while expressing their own concerns about disparities in salaries and conditions of employment between black and white faculty.

We summarize the contents of the memorandum below:

The key concern of the academic staff was that problems at the University of the North could not be isolated from the general discrimination and humiliation suffered by black people outside the University.

The overwhelming majority of the Black students has very deep seated political grievances, and particularly resent the fact that some of their disabilities as Black people are extended and reflected in the administration and in the attitudes of some of the people who run the University.

The Black students deeply resent the fact, for example, that a University for Black people is still firmly in white hands, and that salary disparities and differences in conditions of employment based on race have been institutionalized.

The memorandum affirmed that the majority of the students of the University believe that White academic staff, consisting mainly of Afrikaans-speakers from Afrikaans-speaking universities, do not understand the aspirations of the Black people, and behave and express themselves in a patronizing manner.

The Black Academic Staff Association continued in their memorandum that it is generally submitted that hardly any university exists in the world in which the students do not hold very strong and often passionate political convictions. Indeed it has been said with justification that a community which produces students who are politically apathetic, lacks the idealistic impulse which is essential for the progress of society. In South Africa itself, students at the older universities have at different times expressed themselves forcefully with regard to political matters. White Afrikaner nationalism found very strong and active support at the white Afrikaans universities even in times of war, and more liberalistic expressions of political opinion have come to characterize the student bodies of the white English speaking universities of the Witwatersrand and Cape Town badly because there are opened for black students.

The Black Academic Staff Association continued that there is no reason to expect that students of the University of the North should behave differently or that they must be discouraged in the expression of their idealism. Regard being to the present state of evolution of South Africa's political history, it must be expected that the students of a black university such as University of the North will come to hold strong political convictions. It is respectfully submitted that it would be quite futile to attempt to plan the administration of the University in a manner which will stifle such activity. Expressions of political idealism are inherent in a modern university. The administration of the University is entitled only to require that such expressions are not unlawful, and that academic achievement and performance is not unreasonably impeded. The correctness of both these propositions is accepted as being the common cause.

Of significant was the question in the questionnaire amongst themselves asking: Would you say that sufficient liaison has been established between students and lecturers of your University and those of other universities?

The response to this question was as follows:

1. The Lecturers
The Black and White lecturers operate in such separate orbits that little is known about the degree of association between White lecturers at the University and other

universities. It seems to be clear, however, that such liaison is purely on an ad hoc and unplanned basis, more often associated with the actual interests of the lecturers qua lecturers than the development of thought connected with their respective disciplines. The liaison is not considered to be sufficient or effective.

An Academic Affairs Liaison Committee had been established by the Senate of the University. The Committee was concerned with the selection of speakers from other universities to deliver special lectures at the University. It was believed that whilst this was a useful function, the liaison should ensure the exchange of thought and ideas with other universities on a regular and meaningful ways.

The Black Academic Staff Association then recommended the creation of a nationwide coordinating committee of Black academicians. They hoped that this would lead to a more effective liaison among universities.

2. The Students
The Black Academic Staff Association indicated that students of the University have always been encouraged to meet students at other universities, to exchange ideas and perhaps even to discuss their disagreements. Meeting and talking is an important exercise in instilling a democratic temperament. The Association reasoned that students of the University of the North have both formal and informal contacts with students of other Black universities. The formal contacts had been through the South African Students' Organisation. The Association added that since Tiro's speech, students of the University

of the North had not been allowed to join the South African Students' Organisation because the University authorities believed that the Organisation espoused the "harmful" philosophy of Black consciousness.

The Black Academic Staff Association as it can be assessed in the summaries of the memorandum above was just a flip side of black consciousness. Where the black consciousness was made to be a militant philosophy by the students of the University of the North, the Black academic lectures of the University through the Black Academic Association tried to rationalize and tone it down to suit the academic tastes.

At the centre of the Black Academic Staff was the principle of africanisation of the University. An awareness of the black person as a person capable of managing his own affairs including his own university. In this way the Black Academic Staff of the University of the North elevated the Black Consciousness discourse. They saw Black Consciousness not merely a methodology or a means towards an end. What Black Consciousness seeks to do is to produce at the output end of the process real black people who do not regard themselves as the appendages to white society.

It was this kind of situation that Steve Biko had in mind when he expressed in his column, "I Write what I Like" in the *SASO Newsletter,* his objection to "the intellectual arrogance of white people that makes them believe that white leadership is *a sine qua non* in this country and that whites are divinely appointed pace-setters in progress," and his conviction that black people in South Africa could not be liberated until they are united to break their chains of servitude.

Similar thoughts could also be found in the Black churches in the United States. The Trinity United Christian Church in Chicago in which Barack Obama was a member for twenty years (from 1988 to 2008) asserts that:

> We are a congregation which is Unashamedly Black and Unapologetically Christian... Our roots in the Black religious experience and tradition are deep, lasting and permanent. We are an African people, and remain true to our native land, the mother continent, the cradle of civilization. God has superintended our pilgrimage through the days of slavery, the days of segregation, and the long night of racism. It is God who gives us the strength and courage to continuously address injustice as a people, and as a congregation. We constantly affirm our trust in God through cultural expression of a Black worship service and ministries which address the Black Community.

The Church ascribes to the Black Value System. The Black Value System pledges:

- to Make the Fruits of All Developing and Acquired Skills Available to the Black Community.
- to Allocate Regularly, a Portion of Personal Resources for Strengthening and Supporting Black Institutions.
- allegiance to All Black Leadership Who Espouse and Embrace the Black Value System.

- personal commitment to Embracement of the Black Value System. To measure the worth and validity of all activity in terms of positive contributions to the general welfare of the Black Community and the Advancement of Black People towards freedom.

The fact that the Black Academic Staff Association arose from the solidarity of black students was an awakening. There had been many assertions in the past that there would be no unity amongst blacks because they hold each other in contempt.

The goals of Black Consciousness are to correct false images of Blacks in culture, education, religion, and economics.

Chapter 8:

Pressures exerted on the apartheid State and the Decline of the University of the North

It can be seen clearly from afore chapters that the University of the North was one of those institutions that were at the forefront of the struggle against white domination in South Africa. That struggle begun from its inception and culminated in the 1990s when the National Party under the leadership of FW De Klerk succumbed from increasing pressures. The pressures were local and international. Locally you had the University of the North being one of those catalysts forging coordination and ideological direction giving the black people an intellectual forum where black can come together for debates and discussions around the issues that make them disable in their country. Also through out the continent of Africa signs were everywhere that the apartheid government of South Africa can not be sustained another further.

By the 1990s almost all the countries in Africa have achieved independents from white minority rule. Julius Nyerere of Tanzania spearheaded the formation of a regional bloc called Southern African Development Coordinating Conference (SADCC). SADCC was a loose alliance of nine majority-ruled States in Southern Africa known as the Southern African Development Coordination Conference (SADCC), with the main aim of coordinating development projects in order to lessen economic dependence on the then apartheid South Africa. The founding Member States are: Angola, Botswana, Lesotho, Malawi, Mozambique, Swaziland, United Republic of Tanzania, Zambia and Zimbabwe.

SADCC was formed in Lusaka, Zambia on April 1, 1980, following the adoption of the Lusaka Declaration - Southern Africa: Towards Economic Liberation.

The Organisation of African Unity OAU issued a declaration in 1987 resolving and committing themselves with renewed determination and vigour o the dismantling of the apartheid state in South Africa. Below is the declaration:

Assembly of Heads of State and Government, Twenty-third Ordinary Session, Addis Ababa, Ethiopia, 27-29 July 1987

DECLARATION ON SOUTHERN AFRICA

We, the Heads of State and Government of the Organization of African Unity meeting in our Twenty-third Ordinary Session in Addis Ababa, Ethiopia from 27 to 29 July 1987, Noting with grave concern that the situation in Southern Africa continues to deteriorate,
Having reviewed the exceedingly serious and volatile situation in Southern Africa resulting from the policies of state terrorism, military occupation, blackmail, and the armed bandits by the apartheid regime to destabilize,

sabotage and destroy the economic and social infrastructure of the Frontline States and other countries neighboring it with the aim of weakening and subjugating them,

Recognizing, more than ever before, the urgent need for concerted international action, both short-term and long-term and to provide relief to the Frontline and other States in the region to enable them to withstand the effects of retaliatory sanctions, aggression and destabilization by the South African regime,

1. Observe with serious concern that the Peoples of South Africa and Namibia are subjected to extreme repression and those who fight for liberation become victims of assassination by secret murder squads. Tens of thousands are arrested, detained and tortured and that those South Africans and Namibians, granted refuge in the neighbouring States, are themselves daily targets of this campaign of terrorism and murder;

2. Note with extreme indignation that during and since the racist Whites-only elections of May 6, 1987, the Frontline States have been subjected to intensified and wanton acts of aggression and destabilization carried out both by the Pretoria army and its surrogate bandit forces. They vehemently condemn the barbaric massacre of 400 innocent women, children and elderly at Homoine in Mozambique by the South Africa sponsored and backed armed bandits which exemplifies the barbaric nature of this criminal policy;

3. Condemn positioning by the racist regime of thousands of its soldiers and large quantities of war material on the border between Angola and the occupied territory of Namibia with the objective of assisting the armed UNITA bandits to carry out acts of terrorism against the Angolan people and to establish a zone of military occupation within the territory of Angola;

4. Express our satisfaction with the important measures taken by the Nordic and some Western countries to come to the assistance of the peoples of Southern Africa by imposing sanctions against the Pretoria regime, aiding the liberation movements, and extending economic assistance to the Frontline and SADCC countries;

5. Feel extremely perturbed that the major Western powers continue to aid and abet the Pretoria regime contrary to the wishes and demands of the people of South Africa, Namibia, the region as a whole and the international community;

6. Reject the imposition of unacceptable conditions by the Senate of the United States of America on possible aid to the Frontline and SADCC countries and strongly abhor the attempt by the Senate of the United States of America to associate SADCC with terrorism;

7. Warmly salute the gallant peoples of Southern Africa who, despite all odds, are fighting resolutely to bring about the total liberation of Africa. In this connection we uphold their right to struggle by all means at their disposal – including armed struggle - to achieve their liberation. We reaffirm the unwavering commitment of the OAU to the struggle to eliminate this last vestige of colonialism and White minority domination in our continent;

8. Support the immediate creation of a Pan-African Association of Writers as a valuable contribution to the mobilization of African and world public opinion in the struggle against apartheid;

9. Call upon Member States of our Organization which have not yet created national committees against apartheid to do so and encourage the creation of a Pan-African Association of these national committees.

10. Commit ourselves by common consent to promote specific measures to dismantle apartheid which is the major cause of violence and instability in the region.

To understand the principal stand the OAU had on apartheid government in South Africa one has to consider the fact that South Africa was not a member of the OAU and that the ANC, the apartheid state's most feared liberation movement was often invited to the gatherings of African Heads of States. The ANC in such gatherings were represented by none other than their imminent president Oliver Tambo.

Within this context the OAU was in solidarity with the ANC and it considered the ANC as a government of South Africa. This can be seen clearly by looking at the following paper Oliver Tambo delivered at the OAU:

STATEMENT TO THE OAU LIBERATION COMMITTEE, ARUSHA, FEBRUARY 10, 1983

Your Excellency, Hon. Mr. Edem Kodjo, Secretary-General of the OAU,

Honourable Ministers,

Your Excellencies,

Comrades representatives of the Liberation Movements,

Mr. Chairman,

My first duty is the pleasant one of conveying to this 40th Session of the OAU Coordinating Committee for the

Liberation of Africa the greetings of all our people in South Africa, including especially the leaders and militants of our struggle who are being held in enemy prisons - leaders who, but for their capture, would be participating at this meeting.

Mr. Chairman,

Our meeting takes place at a critical time for our continent. We are at a moment in our history when a coincidence of circumstances has conspired to test our resolve to remain loyal to the objectives set by the founding fathers of the OAU and therefore of this august Committee. The current situation poses to all of us the question - do we have the determination to honour, in struggle, the memory of countless African patriots who sacrificed and perished for the accomplishment of their objectives. It demands that we ask ourselves whether our common determination to win is being translated into a victorious united offensive.

The continent of Africa today carries a primary responsibility to defend the enormous success it has achieved over the last two decades and beyond. The reality of those successes is not in doubt. We cannot forget that only a few decades ago, Africa was described in supercilious tones as the Dark Continent.

However through their heroic efforts, the people of Africa rent asunder the veil of darkness that colonial and imperialist domination had draped over the continent. Acting as self-confident and conscious makers of history, as liberators, we, the offsprings of the so-called Dark Continent, destroyed and buried an entire historical epoch that had been imposed on the peoples of the universe by the ruling classes of an allegedly enlightened Europe and North America. We who were described as backwards became the midwives of the new social reality of independent people, the reality of the collapse of the colonial system, and confounded those who, having invested themselves with an omnipotent and omniscient personality, had thought such a result impossible, undesirable and even inconceivable.

It is these victories that have so transformed the balance of forces in Africa as to render the total liberation of the continent an approaching reality.

Sincere tribute is due to this Committee, to its member countries and to the parent body - the Organisation of Africa Unity, as well as to Africa's allies, supporters and genuine friends beyond her borders, for the seminal role they have played to ensure these monumental victories.

Today, only two countries on our continent - Namibia and South Africa - remain under colonial and white minority domination. This has given rise to a strategic perspective which leaves no doubt but that the brilliant torch of freedom will soon light every single corner of our great motherland.

But precisely because the protracted struggle for the total decolonisation of the continent has reached its final stage, with Africa poised to place its total weight behind the struggle for the defeat of the Pretoria regime, the latter, supported by its imperialist allies, has mounted a multi-pronged counteroffensive, inspired by the belief that its survival lies in the military, economic and political subjugation and control of African independent and sovereign States, in the dismemberment of the OAU and the Non-Aligned Movement, the isolation of southern Africa from the rest of the continent and the international community, and resort to the tactics of bullying, blackmail and bribery - all this with the ultimate aim of crushing the liberation movement, halting the advance towards the total liberation of Africa, and then proceeding to reverse the historic gains of the African revolution.

This counteroffensive began to unfold in earnest with the accession of Ronald Reagan to the White House. Operating on a global scale, and driven by the same suicidal urge for world domination as was Adolf Hitler, Ronald Reagan set out with boundless vigour to organise a war against the national liberation movement, and against the rights of nations and peoples, especially in the non-aligned community, to choose their own course of development in the exercise of their right of self-determination and independence. The Reagan Administration attracted to its camp forces which included fascists, racists, colonialists, neo-Nazis and Zionists.

The South African regime became a strategic ally, precisely because it is a racist, colonialist, fascist regime; a confirmed enemy of black peoples, a brutal oppressor and exploiter which in three decades has killed, murdered and massacred more people in southern Africa than any other regime. It became an ally precisely because this apartheid regime is universally recognised as the perpetrator of a crime against humanity, and has a bloody record of hostility to the decolonisation of Africa. The alliance with such a regime, proudly proclaimed by Reagan, was an act of unmitigated hostility to Africa and an undeserved slap in the face of humanity.

On the other hand, the apartheid regime found in the Reagan Administration the kind of ally it has sought after for many years and which it now needed badly in the face of the tides of African freedom and independence which were pressing in and closing in upon it, especially as a result of the collapse of Portuguese colonialism, the independence of Zimbabwe, the growing might of SWAPO and the revolutionary upsurge within South Africa itself.

With the much-publicised political, military, economic, technological and moral support of the Reagan Administration, an undeclared war is now raging throughout southern Africa, unleashed by the racist regime against the people and countries of the region. The Pretoria regime is clearly using the period of Reagan's term of office as United States President to make the greatest possible advances in the implementation of its so-called "total strategy" for survival as a minority and colonial regime in Africa. Hence the ferocity of the onslaught on the southern region of Africa. In this war the Pretoria regime's objectives are to compel submission and surrender. This is clear in some of the demands which the Reagan Administration and the Pretoria regime are putting forward as their causa belli in southern Africa.

For example, the persistent demand for the withdrawal of Cuban troops seeks to secure fulfilment of the objectives of the 1975 South African invasion of the People's Republic of Angola. It is, in essence, a demand for the surrender of the sovereignty, which is backed by mounting armed aggression and the continuing occupation of the Angolan territory by South African fascist troops.

The objectives for Namibia are same: Botha has declared that there will be no independence for Namibia as long as there is any danger of a SWAPO election victory. Hence the futile attempt to ensure the liquidation of SWAPO as a condition precedent to the independence of Namibia in terms of Security Council Resolution 435.

It is not withdrawal of Cuban troops they want from the Angolan Government: it is Angola itself. It is not the independence of Namibia they do not want: it is Namibian independence without SWAPO - without the Namibian people, who are SWAPO.

But Africa must not permit or assist in the attempt to stand reality on its head: It is the South African invading and occupying troops which must be withdrawn from the People's Republic of Angola. It is the South African regime and its occupation army that must be withdrawn from Namibia. The South African troops are in Angola to murder, destroy towns and property, ruin the economy and destabilise the country. The Cuban troops are in Angola to protect life and property, and help build what has been destroyed. They are there at the request and with the will of an African independent and sovereign State.

Further, Mr. Chairman, Africa, which is the most interested party on the Namibian question, must not allow the South African regime and the United States Administration to keep the international community hopping from one diversionary issue to another.

In addition, Mr. Chairman, the independence of Namibia is also made conditional upon the prevalence of conditions of stability and "security" for the whole region of southern Africa. But this is seen as impossible without the extermination or expulsion of the ANC from the countries of southern Africa.

In this connection, racist Prime Minister Botha has announced that if African independent States refuse to expel the ANC, he will raid them. If they do not refuse but otherwise fail to remove the ANC, his assassins "will do it for them". Equally, if they refuse to sign a military pact with Pretoria, giving the regime the right to raid or invade whenever it feels entitled to do so, then the regime will use its armed forces to compel signature of such a pact. There is no limit to the number of pretexts for armed aggression by the regime, while it lasts, and no let up where there is no surrender.

The world of the Reagan-Botha racist alliance is a lawless world. It constitutes a problem that is at once regional, continental, and even international - a world in which aggression is constantly escalating. How do we deal with this problem?

The solution lies in the achievement of the objectives which have defined the mandate of this Committee since it was established 20 years ago. Hence the heavy responsibilities that rest on the shoulders of the leaders of Africa who are gathered here today. In particular, the solution lies in the eviction of the apartheid colonial regime from Namibia and its destruction within South Africa. Peace and stability are not possible in southern Africa, and indeed in other parts of Africa, while racist and colonial domination continues to hold sway in South Africa and Namibia.

The situation demands, as a matter of urgency, a greatly heightened offensive by the popular masses and PLAN and Umkhonto we Sizwe within Namibia and South Africa respectively. With the current intensification of armed attacks by SWAPO and the Namibian masses, the racists are beginning to find that while they busy themselves with the slaughter of Angolan women and children, their bases are burning in Namibia.

It is however also urgent and important that determined measures be adopted to strengthen the defensive capacity of the southern African independent States and enable them to repulse the aggression of the Pretoria regime.

Africa is pledged to the total liberation of our continent. Accordingly, she has an obligation to continue to mobilise the necessary political and material resources to ensure that this objective is achieved in Namibia and South Africa. The OAU, itself an eminent product of Africa's liberation, remains the one vehicle we have at our disposal to coordinate and mobilise this continental effort aimed at the completion of the task of finally expunging colonialism and racist domination from our continent, consolidating our independence and proceeding with our development programme.

Mr. Chairman,

I started by acknowledging the great victories won by the people of Africa. It is no exaggeration - it is not being alarmist, to say that those victories are now under serious threat, not least because Africa's own capacity to defend them has been seriously impaired by problems - in no way inseparable - which threaten the OAU with at least a partial paralysis. The situation in southern Africa, which has fundamental implications for the future of our continent and for its ability to contribute effectively to the solution of international problems, demands that the OAU must live. The OAU must be strong. It must remain a force with sufficient authority to lead Africa in a victorious assault upon the bastions of colonialism and war that are still entrenched in southern Africa. The OAU must have the capacity to face the future of our continent.

The responsibility to restore the OAU to state of combat-readiness rests on the leaders of our continent who are surely no less illustrious nor any less loyal to the African cause than those who, 20 years ago this year, assembled in Addis Ababa to register one of the greatest achievements in the history of Africa.

The political and military struggle within South Africa continues to grow in its scope and intensity. Ever-increasing numbers of our people are being drawn into active struggle around both local and national issues. Our popular army, Umkhonto we Sizwe, basing itself among, and being part and parcel of, these struggling masses, has established itself as a force equal to the challenges of our situation and much feared by racist Pretoria.

The black section of the working class retains its militancy, is becoming better organised and is growing in its operational capacity as a leading contingent of the liberation forces in South Africa.

Despite the gravely erroneous position recently taken by the "Coloured" Labour Party Congress, opposition to the so-called constitutional proposals is growing. We call for denunciation of these measures.

Details of the situation in South Africa are contained in reports already submitted and placed before this session by the ANC.

Mr. Chairman,

We pledge that the African National Congress, the oppressed and democratic masses in South Africa, will fight on, spear in hand, through thick, through thin, till victory is won for our country, for Africa, for humanity. And let this session of the Liberation Committee signal that the continent of Africa has crossed the Rubicon and has gone over to an uninterrupted offensive which will, within this decade, see the flags of liberation flying over Windhoek, and even over Pretoria.

Thank you.

International Pressures and Isolation of the apartheid state

At the same time, the South African regime has faced growing isolation in the United Nations and other international organizations. It was also becoming increasingly isolated even from States which had formerly given it comfort and confidence, as a result of their recognition of the new realities, the development of anti-racist public opinion in the world and the diplomatic efforts of the OAU and the United Nations Special Committee against Apartheid.

Developments at the United Nations

For the first time, at the 29th session of the General Assembly in 1974, the Credentials Committee decided to reject the credentials of the South African delegation. On 30 September 1974 the General Assembly approved the report of the Credentials Committee by 98 votes to 23, with 14 abstentions.

On the same day, an African Group proposal calling upon the Security Council to review the relationship between the United Nations and South Africa "in the light of the constant violation by South Africa of the principles of the Charter and the Universal Declaration of Human Rights" - was adopted by 125 votes to one (South Africa), with nine abstentions (France, Iran, Israel, Malawi, Nicaragua, Paraguay, Spain, United Kingdom and the United States). Many of the States which found it difficult, because of procedural consideration to support the rejection of credentials, voted for this resolution which declared, in effect, that South Africa had no right to membership in the United Nations: these included the Nordic countries, most EEC countries, Japan, Australia and New Zealand. The vote was a great victory for the African Group and its friends.

A proposal for expulsion was then "brought up in the Security Council, as decided by the Council of Ministers in Mogadishu. There was an impressive debate , with the participation of numerous African and non-African delegations. The proposal received more than the required majority and the three Western Powers were forced to exercise their veto.

What was significant was not the failure of the proposal, which was expected, but the fact that it received wide support, including the positive votes of Australia and Peru. The Western Powers were put under great pressure and felt obliged to give assurances that they would exercise their influence toward meaningful change.

Then came the President's ruling in the General Assembly on 12 November 1974 that the South African delegation cannot participate in the work of the Assembly. The ruling was upheld by 91 votes to 22, with 19 abstentions. This action was unprecedented in the United Nations.

Meanwhile, on 3 October, the General Assembly decided, without a vote, to invite the African National Congress of South Africa and the Pan Africanist Congress of Azania, to participate in the debate on apartheid as observers in the Special Political Committee.

The Assembly was able to take a series of decisions on apartheid, Namibia and the colonial problems by consensus, since South Africa's only consistent ally, Portugal, had deserted her. The 29th session of the General Assembly was thus able to record a great advance in the struggle against apartheid and colonialism in that important international forum.

Equally significant was the fact that the Security Council adopted a resolution on Namibia on 17 December 1974 by a unanimous vote, thus depriving the South African regime of any comfort it may have derived from the vetoes of the Western Powers on the proposal for expulsion.

Developments in the Specialized Agencies of the United Nations

The specialized agencies - especially the UNESCO, ILO, FAO and WHO - have taken further actions, as a. result of the initiatives of the Special Committee against Apartheid or proposals of their members, not only to exclude South Africa but also to join in the campaign against apartheid and support the victims of apartheid and their liberation movements.

The UNESCO has published a source-book on South Africa for use in schools, based on material supplied by the British Anti Apartheid Movement. The ILO has encouraged action by trade unions against apartheid. The WHO has published a study on the effects of apartheid on health, which has received wide publicity. The FAO has agreed to prepare a study on the crucial problem of landownership in South Africa.

Several agencies have initiated educational and other programmes of assistance to the liberation movements, under UNDP grants.

A noteworthy feature is the involvement of agencies which had not in the past shown much activity - because of the weighted votes of Western members or the technical nature of their mandates.

In September 1974, for the first time, South Africa lost its seat on the Board of Directors of the International Monetary Fund and the International Bank, after Australia and New Zealand decided to "break their association with South Africa and no other members were willing to enter into similar arrangements. The defeat was described by the South African press as a "disaster" and a "humiliation".

The Universal Postal Union has decided to exclude South Africa from all conferences.

Several specialized agencies have invited the liberation movements to participate in their meetings.

Actions by States and Organizations

At the same time, there has been a trend toward more concerted action against apartheid by an increasing number of States and public organizations.

For instance, Australia and New Zealand, which had close relations with South Africa, became active opponents of apartheid since the end of 1972. The United Kingdom Government decided, at the end of 1974, to terminate the Simonstown agreement, the only military agreement to which South Africa is a party. The Federal Republic of Germany in 1973 and the United Kingdom in 1974 declared South Africa's administration in Namibia illegal. There have been notable advances in actions by Japan, Lebanon, Mexico, Netherlands and many other countries.

Since 1973, at the invitation of the Special Committee against Apartheid, some of the Western Powers began to co-sponsor and even take the lead in the General Assembly in moving proposals on apartheid, especially as regards release of political prisoners and United Nations efforts to counteract South African propaganda. Contributions to funds for assistance to victims of apartheid increased rapidly. The boycott by Western Powers of the United Nations committees on southern Africa has ended.

The adoption of the International Convention for the Suppression and Punishment of Apartheid signaled a new stage in the uncompromising struggle against apartheid.

There was also a significant advance in public action against apartheid, especially in Western countries. The sports boycott against South Africa has scored new successes. Trade union action against apartheid, was encouraged by the International Conference of Trade Unions against Apartheid, held in Geneva in June 1973. Anti-apartheid movements in Western Europe have launched joint campaigns against emigration to South Africa and collaboration with South Africa. With the liberation of Mozambique and Angola, many public organizations are increasingly focusing their activities on the support to the liberation movements in South Africa, Namibia and Zimbabwe. These campaigns have been encouraged by the Special Committee against Apartheid, the Special Committee on Decolonization and the Council for Namibia.

The new outward policy
The South African regime became concerned - especially after the agreement between Portugal and FRELIMO and the moves for expulsion from the United Nations - that it might be deserted even by its friends among the Western Powers. It increased the military budget by 50 per cent and frantically looked for means to counteract the growing isolation.

It revived, with some variations, the "outward policy" which had been launched by Mr. Vorster in 1967, and which had collapsed by 1971. As Dr. Piet Koornhof, the Minister of Sports, said on 11 November, it decided that: "The way for South Africa to come to terms with the world is via Africa." The priorities had changed.

It hoped to persuade at least some of the independent African States to soften their hostility against apartheid, by:

a. Offering to persuade the Rhodesian regime to release prisoners and negotiate with the African leaders;
b. responding to the concern of African States for the security and development of Mozambique and Angola;
c. taking advantage of the economic difficulties of some African States and offering assistance; and
d. convincing them that it would undertake some improvement in the miserable conditions of the Black people, if given time to persuade its white supporters.

Its main purpose was to persuade African States to abandon their commitment to support the liberation movements in underground activity and armed struggle. Its offers in return were, however, far short of meaningful progress towards independence and full equality.

The South African Foreign Minister, in a speech on 6 November, referred to the triple veto which saved South Africa's membership in the United Nations and said that even the nations which vetoed the proposal had reservations about South Africa's racial policies. "I would be neglecting my duty," he said, "if I did not warn of how dangerous the situation is. How long can we still depend on the Western world to support us?" He appealed to the white supporters of the regime to understand that South Africa must urgently alter the image which African States had of its race policy by removing unnecessary and irritating measures of discrimination.

The various statements of Prime Minister Vorster since October 1974 must be seen as part of this strategy, aimed at changing the image in Africa by removing "unnecessary pinpricks" against the Blacks at home. It is significant that a prominent role in the implementation of this strategy was played by the Secretary of the Department of Information, Dr. Eschel Rhoodie, who managed to visit some African States. The propaganda machinery tried to build up Mr. Vorster as a reasonable man interested in peace. It tried to persuade Governments and others concerned that it is untimely to exert any pressures on the South African regime as it needed goodwill to convince the white electorate to accept reforms.

Mr. Vorster began his offensive with great hopes. He declared on 5 November that if political commentators did not create complications "they will be surprised at where the country will stand in 6 to 12 months time."

But he encountered serious difficulties, except perhaps in the field of propaganda where he was aided by exaggerated press accounts. His successes in the first six months of the offensive have not been impressive.

In Zimbabwe, the Ian Smith regime, in its desperation, engaged in provocative moves which have denied him the image of a peacemaker. In Namibia, the continued resistance of the people belied his pretensions. The offer of the Nationalist Party to have discussions with other "ethnic groups" found hardly any response; the manoeuvres to disrupt the Unity of the Namibians misfired; and the rigging of the elections in Ovambo in January 1975 became a scandal.

In South Africa itself, the removal of "petty apartheid" measures created little impression. Mr. Vorster held several meetings since November with the "leaders" of the bantustans and other apartheid institutions, but even they were obliged to resist being merely used for his purposes.

For, the South African regime had no intention of ending racial discrimination in the country, and soon admitted this in the face of demands that the protestations abroad be reflected in meaningful action in South Africa. Dr. Connie Mulder, the Minister of Interior and Information, announced on 12 November that the policy of contacts with other countries was "within the framework of separate development."

"To ask from us that we must overthrow our whole policy of separate development and give majority rule and integration is totally out of context. That is not our intention and we refuse to do it."

Mr. Vorster himself said on 16 November:

"I want to say... to all the leaders of the Black people: if there are people who are arousing your hopes that there will one day be one-man-one-vote in the white Parliament for you, then they are misleading you, because that will never happen."

It is significant that even some "bantustan leaders have expressed little enthusiasm for Mr. Vorster's new outward policy.

After the news of Mr. Vorster's visit to Liberia, Chief Lucas Mangope, leader of the bantustan of Bophuthatswana, said on 19 February:

"Mr. Vorster and his men should first tackle more urgent issues concerning blacks in South Africa."

Dr. Cedric Phataudi, leader of the bantustan of Lebowa, said:

"it would be unfortunate if Mr. Vorster built up his foreign policy at the cost of his home policy with blacks of South Africa ..." (The Times, London, 20 February 1975).

Reforms within the apartheid state

The South African regime has been trying to convince the world that it has embarked on efforts to improve the position of the Black majority. According to its propaganda, the first stage of apartheid (or "separate development") was segregation to remove friction among racial groups and was, therefore negative. The second stage which has now begun is development of bantustans and local government bodies for the Coloured people and Indians - which is positive. Irritating measures which are unnecessary for maintaining white identity and white domination (in six-seventh of the country) can now be removed.

This policy, at best, offers no equality. It means a partition of the country under which the white minority will appropriate six-sevenths of the rich resources of the country and ask the majority of the people to be satisfied with the rest and depend on the charity of the whites. All the Black leaders and organizations in the country, including even most of those who have agreed to work within the apartheid system, have rejected the regime's offers.

A review of some of the recent "reforms", which have been highly publicized by the regime and its friends, shows that they are the result of pressure from within the country and internationally, and do not represent meaningful progress towards equality.

The University of the North in the light of these developments

The 1990s as a watershed for the realization of the struggle against white minority rule in South Africa was to have significant impact to the University of the North. The University as we have seen throughout was like an intellectual battalion against apartheid through its student body and eventually the Black Academic Staff

Association. These had great influence to the evolution of the University. The University became famous not because of the formal education students receives in the lecture halls but through its student body which has mobilized itself into a political bloc throughout the existence of the University. One can reason that activities and culture of university students can not form the foundation of a university since students do not stay long at university - a larger part of students spent three to four years at the university and after graduation leave the university. So with those brief years of student stay at university one may argue that students contribution to the university culture is fragile and flimsy. But that was not the case at the University of the North as students were mobilized through highly effective mass meetings where political debates were taking place and memos, letters and resolutions against the apartheid states were drawn out. The resolutions and the memos were not directed to the University administration, often in many instances the memos, letters and resolutions were directed to the South African president himself bypassing the University administration and the Department of Education.

These established student practices and tradition was to weave together a generation of students together as one and in turn psychologically influencing the whole University establishment as a University against the apartheid state. This is the badge and brand which the University of the North is generally know about. It was a University for indigenous black people with a intellectual fighting culture against the apartheid state.

So the dismantling of apartheid meant that the University of the North was being "dismantled". That means if there is no apartheid anymore it therefore should mean that there should not be a University of the North. So in the 1990s the University gradually started to loose significance. This aspect was to reach tipping point with Nelson Mandela the president of the ANC and ultimately of the country started preaching reconciliation between the white and black people of South Africa. In this reconciliation it was observed by many and it was often seen as black compromising their stand against white people. That black people should open their arms for white people while white people only paid lip service to the reconciliation without any significant ideological shifts of their perception of black people.

So the University as was known through its student's protests continued to voice their concerns and the fact that because liberation movements have been unbanned by the apartheid government it does not meant that the struggle is over. There is still a need for creating an environment for a new South Africa first by blacks and presenting this model to the rest of South Africans. This in its face value contradicted Nelson Mandela's reconciliation project of embracing the whites. A note here can also be made of the fact of black consciousness which its features with the concerned of the black person not South Africa as such. And having seen how the Black Consciouness Movement was entrenched at the University of the North it was not easy that the philosophy of reconciliation as preached by Nelson Mandela would take root easily at the University.

So the culture of protests and fight against the apartheid system continued amongst students even when negotiations or reconciliation was continuing amongst the apartheid state and the liberation movements. The more this contradictions happened, the more people listen to news and read newspapers about students of the University of the North the more the University became anathema, abominations, ridicule and laughing stock of society

These were the seeds of the decline and the near collapse of the University of the North in 1999 where the ANC government was confronted with the reality of the possibility of closing the University.

Chapter 9:

The New University of the North

Is the University of the North of the 21st century still on the cutting edge of black consciousness? To answer this question we look at the years preceding the incorporation of the Medical University of South Africa into the University of the North to create the University of Limpopo.

In 2000, the University of the North found itself in a serious governance crisis. The Principal and Chairperson of Council had been suspended. Many senior University administrators were suspended (with full pay) on charges of corruption and incompetence. Student activity programmes collapsed and members of the Student Representative Council seized the moment to become the kingpins and bosses of the University.

Allegations and counter allegations of corruption were bandied around in the media and on campus.
Acting under the provisions of the Higher Education Act 101 of 1997, Minister of Education Professor Kadar Asmal (former Chairperson of the University Council) appointed Deputy Vice-Chancellor and Vice Principal at the University of Cape Town Professor Thandabantu

Nhlapo, to assess the situation of the University. Professor Nhlapo and his team issued a devastating report, describing the University as *a fallen behemoth with many parasites living off the carcass but with very few of these parasites committed to or even interested in the core business of universities everywhere in the world.*

Professor Nhlapo insisted that the University of the North close down for a significant period. Should that prove impractical, he recommended that the Minister install an administrator under the provisions of the Higher Education Act, with absolute powers to salvage the University.

The Minister unequivocally rejected Professor Nhlapo's recommendation to close down the University. However he did agree to appoint an administrator, and asked for the resignation of the entire council of the University. In January 2001 Professor Patrick FitzGerald, Vice Principal of the University of the Witwatersrand was appointed administrator of the University with full powers of a University Principal.

Professor FitzGerald began by conducting his own assessment of the University. His report identified three challenges for the University: survival; stabilization and sustainability; and becoming entrepreneurial and value adding.
- Professor FitzGerald considered the following strategic and institutional issues:
- Lack of due governance processes and management controls
- Animosity between management, staff unions and students
- Poor public image and low institutional morale

- Declining student enrolments and, therefore, also declining state subsidy
- Increase in student debtors and ongoing student debt
- Annual budgetary deficit
- Dysfunctional academic architecture
- Overstaffed support service component

In developing a solution to these problems Professor FitzGerald was faced with many strategic issues:

Should the main effort be directed towards simply restoring order and functionality of the University, or should he added to the primary task of restoration of functionality seize the opportunity to embark on a major change management exercise, which would fundamentally reposition the University in a new era of an emerging knowledge economy and in the new South African higher education environment?

Professor FitzGerald had to determine the extent to which a reconstructed University of the North could be effective and successful in the emerging contexts of South African, African and global higher education. The existing architecture, attitudes and approaches of the University even if functionally restored seemed unlikely to achieve the outcomes that the South African Government, the community the University served, employers and students demanded. Good governance, proper management and even infrastructure and resource improvements, FitzGerald reasoned, would not significantly reposition the University in line with the exigencies of a highly competitive higher education environment and the modalities of producing the requisite human resources and research knowledge for South Africa's economic and developmental needs.

The choice, therefore for FitzGerald was to attempt to move beyond the classical and conservative premises by which the University of the North had been operating. A new organizational architecture was needed to be designed that would serve as the bedrock and foundation from which the University will develop its potential to provide both general and niche knowledge services to students, government, and industry. Resources needed to be leveraged (intrapreneurial) and far more attuned to building its capacity in line with the needs of and opportunities within its external operating environment (entrepreneurial).

Professor FitzGerald chose to make the University of the North a cutting edge in South Africa. To do this FitzGerald identified intrapreneurial and entrepreneurial developmental issues.

There were some critics to this approach. That a collapsed university such as University of the North was hardly the raw material of a viable entrepreneurial higher education university. All arguments were that FitzGerald should achieve a conventional functioning organization before attempting to steer it into even more complex and uncharted strategic waters.

But FitzGerald argued that a mere technical restoration of obsolete machinery was not strictly an option, since such obsolescence would simply ensure that the University would lurch into yet another strategic and organizational crisis. The current emergency, allowing for legitimate intervention, could provide an opportune moment to transform the University into a well-positioned, strategically aware and entrepreneurial competitive knowledge powerhouse, capable of critical and integral responses to environmental needs and demands.

Reasons for a university not to promote entrepreneurism are many, and include a lack of historical tradition forced by limited mission statements in the institution's history. This lack of entrepreneurism may even have become a self-perpetuating system within which attitudes such as *We've never done it this way before* are well rooted. This problem is due not only from there being few local new venture firms to act as role models for potential entrepreneurs in the academic community, but also because many academic community members with exciting new concepts never even consider that their concepts could result in a commercialized product.

Universities that accomplish their primary mission of teaching and/or research, but do not establish and nurture new venture creation leave untapped a vast resource that could be used for the betterment of their communities.

Establishing a culture of entrepreneurship at a university requires significant energy and resources from institutional, governmental, and private personnel. Decisions must be made to do things differently, either to spend limited resources to nurture early "model ventures" or to spend the resources to create an infrastructure that will nurture many new ventures.

In *Creating Entrepreneurial Universities: Organisational Pathways of Transformation,* Clark (1998) cites the characteristics of entrepreneurial and innovative universities:

- Strong steering core: universities that want to change cannot depend on traditional weak control of steering. They need to become quicker, more flexible and more focused in reacting to demands from their environments.
- A developmental periphery: A university that wants to change need to have mechanisms to relate to the outside world. They have to reach across their traditional boundaries. They may need to set up special organizational units to do so.
- A diversified funding base: universities that want to change need the resources to do so. They specially need discretionary funds. This means that they have to widen their financial base (and become less dependent on subsidies from the government).
- A stimulated academic heartland: Universities that want to change need basic academic units that become the very base of the institution's identity.

FitzGerald found that the University of the North possessed the potential for *a strong steering core* in the form of the administrator. The University possessed inherent strong academic heartland in its emphasis on traditional undergraduate teaching.

With regard to the other three of Clark's criteria, FitzGerald noted that the University of the North failed to meet the benchmarks. Therefore FitzGerald argued that significant strategic thinking, as well as considerable institutional and cultural change would be a prerequisite to the development of entrepreneurial modalities at the University.

A strong steering core

The appointment of Professor FitzGerald provided an opportunity for strong steering and quick strategic reaction in South Africa's rapidly changing higher education sector. FitzGerald had the power to appoint an executive team, which included several outside interim managers, both in an advisory capacity and with authority to transform the positioning, shape and operations of the University.

The Interim Advisory Group which FitzGerald established immediately defined the following institutional objectives for the University:

- Re-establish the core mission of learning, teaching and research
- Install proper management control and institutional governance
- Renew and reconfigure the academic architecture
- Enhance the institutional morale and public image
- Entirely restructure the administrative and support services
- Focus on the improvement of internal efficiencies
- Maximize the student funding framework and invest in growth areas
- Enhance the future revenue productivity
- Review returns generated from assets
- Strategically reposition the University in line with contemporary realities

Rapid progress in regard to some of these objectives was the sine qua non of any turnaround. The purpose of learning, teaching and research which constituted the rationale for the existence of the organization and for its annual receipt of public monies was immediately and forcibly advocated. The University was described, ironically, as an extremely successful employment bureau – as demonstrated by the massive overstaffing and by the employment of scores of people who had little or nothing to do. At another level, the prestige and prerogatives of managers had eclipsed that of academics, to the extent that academics crossed into administrative positions in order to enjoy the prestige, remuneration, and working conditions.

Institutional morale was low, and much was expected from FitzGerald to raise it.

FitzGerald observed though that despite all problems the University remained the top historically black university in the number of peer reviewed journal articles that its faculty published. The University also possessed centers of excellence in mathematics, physics, materials modeling, agricultural science, education and law. Therefore, FitzGerald argued that strategic steering could be used to bolster and shape a strong academic heartland on the basis of the comparative advantages that the University already possessed.

FitzGerald contended that even stronger steering needed to be applied to the public image or brand of the University. Although the academic and organizational situation at University of the North was no worse, and in certain respects was considerably more favorable than, many South African universities – black and white.

FitzGerald attributed the University's poor public image to unflattering newspaper coverage. The University had been regarded as the center of Black intellectualism and its status as a leader in the struggle against the apartheid government led to its collapse.

FitzGerald therefore considered an intensive public relations campaign, starting with key stakeholders, donors and partners, and spreading to the regional and national media.

Fitzgerald noted that the informal, but universal use of the name "Turfloop" or "Turf" in reference to the University had been eschewed by previous management, presumably because of Turfloop had been the name of the farm on which the University sat.

At the same time, the term conjured the proud spirit of the University as a center of black intellectual struggle against apartheid and racism. FitzGerald coined the motto *Come to the University of the North and Learning is our Turf.* The motto was quickly instituted to link the memory of a proud black heritage in South Africa to the University's important role in the future of South African higher education.

A technological developmental periphery

Fitzgerald identified several sites and issues that needed to be developed. It concerned him that the computer laboratories closed at 16h00 during the week and were closed on weekends and public holidays. In addition, several laboratories fell under the control of departments that opened them only for their own students, and some of these went unused for weeks or even months. Students who did not study computer-related subjects were not encouraged to use the IT facilities.

FitzGerald notes that some University staff opposed expanding access to the computer laboratories. They contended that personnel could not be expected to supervise the facilities after hours without generous overtime pay, and that unsupervised student assistants could not be trusted to manage the laboratories. Staff also claimed that students would abuse the facilities and that there was insufficient bandwidth for so many students to access the Internet simultaneously.

However FitzGerald eventually won the battle and the computer laboratories were kept open until 18h00, then until 20h00 and then 22h00; they were also available for use on weekends. Student assistants were paid to staff the labs at student work rates, and by bursary students who owed a number of hours of service to the University.

As a result of these new policies, the computer labs were filled to capacity. A year after this new arrangement not a single incident of abuse by student assistants had been reported and no damage to computers had occurred beyond normal wear and tear.

FitzGerald states that academics and managers continued to allege that students were not really using the computers properly, but spent all the time visiting music and other non-academic sites, even though University software controls automatically blocked pornographic and other undesirable addresses. However, FitzGerald noted that monitoring and his own random visits to the laboratories revealed that the vast majority of students were using the computers and the Internet for study and research.

At about that time a dispensation was negotiated between Telkom (South Africa's only fixed-line provider), the South African Universities Vice-Chancellors Association, through the establishment of the Tertiary Education Network, and a major United States foundation, to provide increased Internet bandwidth at a steep discount. The impact, after an affordable hardware investment by the University was a more than 1 000 per cent increase in available bandwidth.

The combined effect of these measures, FitzGerald notes, was a sea change in the student information and communication culture. Walk-in access to Internet and e-mail transformed the climate at the University from being locked in the *bundu* to being in touch with national and global news, information, and knowledge. A small and inexpensive intrapreneurialism was thus able to level the playing fields between students at the University of the North and at top-tier universities around the world. Consequently learning and knowledge at the University advanced its connectedness to the world beyond the campus, and generated the consciousness of a developmental periphery that was strategically linked to university activities.

ACCEPTANCE SPEECH BY THE DEPUTY PRESIDENT, JACOB ZUMA, ON RECEIVING AN HONORARY DOCTORATE FROM THE UNIVERSITY OF THE NORTH, Pietersburg, 13 October 2001

Ladies and Gentlemen
I cannot even begin to put into words how I feel about being afforded the distinction of being awarded an honorary doctorate by such an illustrious institution.

I feel particularly privileged by your decision, especially since I follow in the footsteps of eminent statesmen and giants of the African liberation struggle such as the late ANC President Oliver Tambo, Former President Nelson Mandela, the late Dr Mwalimu Nyerere and Dr Kenneth Kaunda.

The fact that this institution honored leaders of the caliber mentioned shows sound political judgment and clear direction.

Cde Tambo, an honourary doctorate of this university was an intellectual giant who dedicated his whole life to the freedom of his people, and sadly did not live to see the consolidation of the freedom he fought for.

You also honored Madiba, a highly regarded international statesman and an asset to this country and its people. In addition, Dr Kaunda and Dr Nyerere opened up their hearts and countries to South Africans and provided us with support that can never be quantified.

It is also important to note that this institution has produced many outstanding people who are now leaders in business, government and political parties in this country, from the ANC to other political formations. Distinguished guests, I must also state that I believe this award has not been given to me as an individual. I am therefore receiving it on behalf of the collective - my comrades in the ANC, with whom I have shared the trenches in exile and in prison, and with whom I still toil to ensure that the quality of life of South Africans is improved.

I am also accepting this doctorate on behalf of all the unsung heroes and heroines of the Northern Province. May they, through this honor, know that their contribution to the liberation of this country is valued. In addition, it is indeed a privilege for me to be honored by this institution in particular, given the role it has played in our country. Having been established under apartheid as a *Bush College* it has managed to survive against all odds, and has made a sterling contribution to our history.

During the darkest days of apartheid, Turfloop became a terrain of struggle, and for that reason, the history of student resistance would be incomplete without the recording of the role played by this university.

It was also in this institution that the South African Students Organisation (SASO) was formed in 1969. The resistance raged on through the seventies and eighties and many, including Abraham Tiro to name but one, paid the ultimate price. The proceedings of the graduation ceremony of 1972 are well known, where Abraham Tiro made his historic provocative speech, which led to his expulsion.

This institution has indeed come a long way, and it has a rich history. The challenge is now to move on and meet the challenges of the new economy and New World order.

Already, this University is well known as an important centre of learning, research and teaching. Currently, this expertise is being developed further in the field of enhancing indigenous knowledge systems.

You have correctly taken advantage of your rural locality over the years and produced outstanding research. These innovations in many fields must be encouraged to continue. I'm pleased to learn that some disciplines like Biotechnology and Nutrition are working or have completed research on how the morula, mopani and other indigenous plants can be used to sustain healthy diets for people, particularly in the rural areas.

This focus on indigenous knowledge systems will give us a competitive edge over other institutions beyond our borders. Such research should filter across the board to produce an integrated study in other disciplines, like law for instance. I have in mind here a school of law, which can correctly integrate the indigenous law system of lekgotla/imbizo with the modern day law and see how those can be used to develop a curriculum that is grounded within its African reality.

Sociology, Anthropology, Mathematics, Health Sciences, Philosophy and other subjects can also be found to be indebted to indigenous knowledge systems.

Ladies and gentlemen, still on the point of rural development, I hope you are aware of the Integrated Sustainable Rural Development Programme (IRSDP) that was launched by government on 7 July 2001. The aim of the programme is to make rural areas socially and economically viable. Our programme is focused on getting rural communities to move away from subsistence modes of basic economic activities to productive, sustainable and growth enhancing economic activities.

The institution would be well placed to participate in this important rural development within the province and the region.

Such a role would further entrench this university in the community, as universities in the developing world need to position themselves as an integral part of communities they serve. I have been informed that Turfloop is attempting to achieve that connectivity. An example is the recent launch of computer laboratories by the Minister of Communications. It is encouraging indeed to see the university responding to the needs of the communities around it. Such well-equipped laboratories should, if possible be the centre of development of information technology in the North and in Mpumalanga.

Ladies and gentlemen, I cannot finish my address without touching on the Millennium African Recovery Programme, also known as the New African Initiative. The Organisation of African Unity endorsed the programme in August this year.

The objective is to place the countries of the continent on a path of sustainable growth and development so that we can take our rightful place in the world in this, the African Century.

This Initiative is a pledge by African leaders, based on a common vision and firm conviction to eradicate among other things, conflicts, poverty and disease and bring about democracy, peace and stability and promote trade and investments.
Turfloop is correctly situated in the Southern African Development Community (SADC) region to contribute to the recovery programme.

I am therefore pleased to hear that this institution is already forming linkages with other institutions in the continent. The Turfloop Graduate School of Leadership, I noticed, has in the past months started forging links with universities and institutions in East Africa through the Indigenous Knowledge Programme.

These collaborations will see us sharing knowledge and skills and enhance co-operation to develop our region and continent.

Distinguished guests, in as much as we can talk about Africa's development we should also critically begin to ponder on how we can offer ourselves to the service of our country.

In that spirit, I would like to challenge all gathered here, especially the graduands, to begin the process of skills and knowledge transfer through voluntarism. This concept is not new to us; it has always been part of our tradition.

As we graduate today, we need to ask ourselves what it is that we can do to make the lives of people in our communities better. I am convinced that we are all up to the challenge.

Master of ceremonies, once again, let me stress that I am truly humbled and honoured by this recognition by the University of the North.

I wish you all the best in all your endeavours in this fine institution with a rich heritage.

I thank you.

Chapter 10:

University of Limpopo: A True African University in a Globalised World

The following articles first appeared in the Limpopo Leader, a quarterly journal of the University of Limpopo

From Despair to Hope: the Turfloop Experience

In 1997, a university employee, Christopher White, published his doctoral thesis under the title *From Despair to Hope: the Turfloop Experience.* Listen to his description of the institution at that time: 'The University of the North is at an exciting time in its history. It is an institution that has witnessed the anguish of conflict, of deep-seated alienation, distrust and the dilemma of an identity crisis. Power struggles and conflict still prevail, as the University leadership attempts to marry the claims of the statutory and non statutory, the academic and the administrative, the student and the teacher, and the University and the broader community ... As the University grapples with inherent fears and the consequences of change, it should consider the consequences of no change at all.

Society is undergoing fundamental change ... Change is the price of survival. If the system has come to rest at the edge of chaos, an environmental jolt might push it into the abyss of chaos under an avalanche of reinforced change. The University should take up the challenge to become a leader in higher education at the cutting edge of change rather than being forced into unplanned change.'

By the end of the 1990s, Turfloop came close to being closed down. Gradually, however, and with immense difficulty, the University of the North (and now in combination with Medunsa the University of Limpopo) has taken Christopher White's advice. The three interviews that follow give an indication of this difficult passage. They chart the progress of an institution that is now taking charge of its own destiny. They also give an indication of the flavour of the future.

The transformation of higher education:
WHATITMEANSATTURFLOOPTHEUNIVERSITY OF THE NORTH IS NOW REGARDED AS LIMPOPO'S FLAGSHIP UNIVERSITY. But it hasn't all been easy sailing since 1994. After the tensions of the final years of the struggle, when campus unrest and the presence of the military were the order of the day, UNIN entered into a prolonged and often painful interregnum. On campus the closed system of education of the past began to give way to a version of the new open system in wide international currency.

A democratic Council was elected. Nelson Mandela was appointed Chancellor, and the accomplished writer and academic Professor Chabani Manganyi filled the hot seat of on-campus Vice-Chancellor and Principal. A Broad Transformation Committee was formed, and this body played a crucially important role in the urgently required strategic planning process that for the first time deliberately involved all stakeholders and aimed specifically at genuine openness and full accountability. The result was a collectively defined vision and mission statement, as well as a process, initiated by the then Administrator Professor Patrick Fitzgerald in consultation with the Academic Planning Committee, of rationalising the academic structures of the University. In place of the eight old faculties with their 48 departments have emerged three faculties with 11 schools. These are:

The F a c u l t y o f H u m a n i t i e s , containing the schools of
(i)   Languages & Communications;
(ii)   Education; and
(iii)   Social Sciences.

The F a c u l t y o f S c i e n c e , H e a l t h & A g r i c u l t u r e , containing the schools of :
(i)   Computational & Mathematical Sciences
(ii)   Physical & Mineral Sciences
(iii)   Molecular & Life Sciences
(iv)   Health Sciences
(v)   Agricultural & Environmental Sciences

The F a c u l t y o f M a n a g e m e n t S c i e n c e s a n d L a w , containing the schools of:
(i)   Economics & Management;
(ii)   The Turfloop Graduate School of Leadership; and
(iii)   Law.

After a period in the early years of the new century when UNIN was placed under provisional management to establish organisational and financial stability, the Minister of Education announced that he was conferring 'flagship' status on three of the nation's universities that had been historically disadvantaged by the policies of apartheid: the University of the Western Cape; Fort Hare and the University of the North.

Clearly, this honour is in recognition of the will at University to transform itself into one of South Africa's leading universities, regardless of its past. As University's Acting Vice-Chancellor, Professor Mahlo Mokgalong, remarks: 'We know that the flagship tag means that the national Department of Education has confidence in what we are trying to do. We went through our restructuring with the realization that it was no longer feasible to compartmentalize knowledge. Hence the interdisciplinary schools, where an opportunity is constantly provided to contextualise specialist knowledge. But I must say that our flagship status, while strengthening our hand in many fields, will not mean much unless we rise to the challenge and ensure that the epithet fits. The responsibility is with us to search for excellence in research, academic output – in fact in everything we do.'

Few doubt that the University will succeed. On 1 January 2005 the University of the North will merge with the Medical University of South Africa (Medunsa) and the name of the new institution thus created will be the University of Limpopo. 'Our relationships with our grassroots communities, already strong, will increase,' says Professor Mokgalong, 'and these communities – around the campus, all over Limpopo province, and into the SADC countries to the north – will continue to feed their cream into our courses and programmes. Our relationship with government will also be strengthened. Already, we are working extensively with provincial education and agricultural authorities. And important new partnerships are looming with health and mining and a lot more.'

All this is a far cry from the institution that grew out of South Africa's preoccupation with apartheid, and from the 'bush university' taunts of the past. The University at Turfloop now looks like a youthful giant in South Africa's revamped tertiary education sector – and it's standing tall and optimistic for the province whose name it will soon carry.

The great Limpopo merger
UNIN + MEDUNSA = The University of Limpopo

On 1 January 2005 an important event took place that will strengthen the Health Care in Limpopo Province. The chances are that it will do a lot more to Turfloop. Before we attempt an assessment of the effects, however, we need to understand some of the detail of the momentous event itself. The bald fact is this. At the start of the year the University of the North outside Polokwane was officially merged with the Medical University of Southern Africa, situated on the northern edges of Gauteng province, to create a new institution known as the University of Limpopo.

The merging process has been protracted and not without difficulties and unhappiness. Many problems remain to be resolved. But the terms of the notice in the Government

Gazette (number 23549 of 21 June 2002) are unequivocal. *'The Ministry of Education should, in consultation with the new institution, assess, investigate and make decisions on the relocation (over the medium to long term) of Medunsa's programmes and infrastructure to the Northern Province.'*

In simplistic terms, then, Limpopo province is in the process of getting its own fully fledged medical school. This is spectacularly good news for a region that has traditionally been under-endowed – at least from a health care point of view. Consider just one statistic: the doctor/population ratio in the old Lebowa homeland (now a part of Limpopo, of course) was at one time 1:27 000, while in certain parts of Gauteng the parallel ratio was less than 1:500.

Three cheers, then, for a merger that begins to redress such inequities, and whose intent is clearly in line with the national policy of decentralising South Africa's intellectual expertise and academic capacity.

But the process now begun is far from straightforward. There are cons as well as pros. Those people hoping at any moment to see a line of removal vans bringing north all the high-tech paraphernalia of a medical school and tertiary hospital – not to mention the busloads of academics and medical scientists necessary to staff one – will inevitably be disappointed. Equally, those people hoping that the merger will be 'on paper' only, and that the status quo at both the merging institutions will remain undisturbed will be equally so.

The reality is that to merge two institutions is a hugely complex process. To imagine that it will not take time – and patience – would be folly. Nevertheless, the implications for South Africa's most northerly – and most rural – province are enormous.

The fall and rise of an African university
A Visionary leader emerges to steer the ship

At its meeting on the 22 August 2006, the Council of the University of Limpopo resolved that Professor N Mahlo Mokgalong be appointed as the first substantive Vice-Chancellor and Principal of the University of Limpopo. The appointment marks the end of a long period of instability and change in the affairs of the University of the North and the Medical University of Southern Africa. According to the media release announcing the news, 'this Council decision was made mindful of the need for strong management and leadership to guide the University of Limpopo in confronting the many challenges facing the higher education sector. The University of Limpopo has to respond to numerous directives and policy initiatives ... as well as to take the merger (between UNIN and Medunsa) to the next level whereby a Medical Faculty is established in Limpopo'.

But who exactly is this man in the hot seat, and what is his vision? The following pages provide some crucial answers.

MOKGALONG THE MAN
He is from a remarkably tough generation of South Africans.

Consider the following list of names: Cyril Ramaphosa, Frank Chikane, Matthews Phoza, Danisa Baloyi, Yvonne Mokgoro, Mokgadi Mailulu. These key figures in the struggle against apartheid and in post-1994 South Africa were all studying on the Turfloop campus at the same time as Mahlo Mokgalong.

'I was very rapidly politically educated,' he remarks with a smile. 'It was a way of life on the campus. We attended after-hours classes in political education, and we all belonged to SASO (the South African Students Organisation). During my first year on campus, 1972, the SASO national president was Onkgopotse Tiro, and he too was a student at Turfloop. He was later (in May 1972) expelled for his political activities. The early 1970s also marked the height of our awareness of the Black Consciousness Movement that had started in America. We used to do Black Power salutes when we greeted each other.' These admissions jar slightly against Mokgalong's current reality. The newly appointed Vice-Chancellor of one of South Africa's most complex universities dresses in dark suits and is always quietly polite. But his underlying strength, only occasionally glimpsed, was without doubt forged in those heady and dangerous student days. As with many others, the temper of the times in the 1970s and 1980s forced high levels of commitment and maturity early onto his young shoulders. Mokgalong was born in 1954 at Ga-Masemola, a rural village on the road between Lebowakgomo and Jane Furse in Sekhukhuneland. His father was a school principal and his mother managed a family shop. The village has grown substantially since the 1950s, but barefooted children still play among the dwellings.

'I grew up in a family which held education in high esteem,' says Mokgalong, knowing well enough that even then the course of his life was being set. For his own education, he went to live with an aunt at nearby Schoonoord. Remarkably, at the small primary school there one of his earliest friends was a boy called Malegapuru Makgoba who in 2005 was appointed Vice-Chancellor at the University of KwaZulu Natal. To start their high school careers, both boys were sent to Hwiti High School where their new school was within walking distance of the Turfloop campus. No doubt because of this proximity, the boys enjoyed the then rare advantages of being taught by graduate teachers. 'But the campus buildings were a constant reminder to us of the possibilities that the future held,' Mokgalong recalls. 'We used to go onto campus to the sports fields. We were herded along under escort like a flock of sheep. But we never went into the university proper. It was only later, as a student, that I entered a laboratory for the first time in my life and had my first glimpse of an actual microscope.'

It was after matriculating that the two friends from Sekhukhuneland went their separate ways. Makgoba travelled down to Durban to study medicine. Mokgalong gained admittance to Turfloop where he tackled a BSc Biological Sciences degree. In spite of the plentiful political distractions of the time, he cruised through his first degree and added Honours and Master's qualifications in quick succession. By 1977, he had joined the university staff as a research assistant, and was promoted to lecturer not long after he began work on his doctorate in parasitology. 'My research activities took me to many countries,' Mokgalong recalls, 'but I spent most of my time abroad in Finland and also at the Institute of Parasitology in St Albans in England. I spent several three to six month blocks at the Institute, and I loved every moment of it. I saw myself as a scientist and

I saw this as my life. I was happy where I was.' Fate was soon to intervene, however. The great change in Mokgalong's career began innocuously enough. After he had been awarded his doctorate, he was asked to become deputy dean of Turfloop's Faculty of Sciences. Not long afterwards, the dean (Professor Mbudzeni Sibara) was seconded to an outreach campus that had been established in the old homeland of QwaQwa, and Mokgalong found himself in the position of acting dean. 'I could see what was happening and I said to myself: let me give it my best shot because I don't want to see this university fail. Events moved rapidly, and after the academic restructuring under the control of the administrator, I was appointed Executive Dean of the new Faculty of Sciences, Health and Agriculture. But after not much more than a year, I found myself as acting VC of the University. I took over from the administrator – who's powers had been absolute – so the task was like trying to guide this bruised institution in a transition from military back to civilian rule. We had to re-establish virtually all the structures of governance.'

To complicate matters, the merger between the University of the North and Medunsa was announced in December 2002 and planned to take effect at the start of 2005. So Mokgalong's rise to the top position in the merged University of Limpopo began in 2003 and culminated with his appointment in August of 2006. 'In the late 1990s, everyone was disillusioned and unhappy. I interacted with all the constituencies. Throughout my years as acting and intermin VC, it's not that there weren't protests, strikes, and all the rest of it. But I think that what makes a leader is being able to ride the waves. And through all the upheavals – not least those surrounding the merger – I made a point of not keeping any grudges.

After each storm had passed, we were therefore able to pick up the pieces and carry on – for the common good.' This sense of 'the common good' runs powerfully through Mokgalong's perception of leadership, and his perceptions of the future. The common good requires effort to achieve, it requires teamwork, but above all it requires taking responsibility. Listen to Mokgalong's take on what it means to be African.

'Of course, I'm optimistic about Africa. The continent is still going through a recovery process after colonial rule. But I believe it is Africans themselves who must drive the future. We need to get our acts together. If we keep blaming colonialism – and apartheid – we won't get anywhere. Colonialism and apartheid are dead. We have to meet the challenges for ourselves. That's what it means to be African: accepting responsibility for our continent.' Mokgalong, one of Limpopo's brightest sons.

(The following excerpts are taken from Professor Mokgalong's presentation to the Council committee responsible for choosing the new Vice-Chancellor of the University of Limpopo.).

THE VISION of the new University is informed by the recent restructuring of South Africa's higher education institutions through mergers and rightsizing. In December 2002, the Minister of Education announced cabinet's decision to merge the University of the North and the Medical University of Southern Africa. In addition, the new institution was mandated to become one of the three flagship institutions to be created out of previously disadvantaged universities. Cabinet's decision further requires all institutions involved in mergers to prepare institutional operating plans that will give effect to the direction that these institutions will take over the next three to five years.

This presented the University of Limpopo with an opportunity to craft a new vision suitable for a flagship premier African university. The new vision of which I was the architect and now the prime driver ... seeks excellence and global competitiveness. The University has consciously chosen to focus on rural problems within the larger community we serve. This is not to pretend that African rural problems are unique, but rather to focus intellectual energy, financial and material resources to address hitherto largely neglected problems of the rural poor, who the world over have been neglected by universities and other knowledge producers. It is our intention to develop a high-calibre world-class research institution. We should engender a mentality worldwide where, when students want to research rural issues, the University of Limpopo should be their first port of call. Our new motto is 'the University of Limpopo for human and environmental wellness in a rural context: *finding solutions for Africa*'.

Perhaps it is germane that one should reflect how the higher education landscape has transformed worldwide in the 21st century. Gone are the days when academics were cloistered in their ivory towers, dreaming about the stars and the heavens with scant regard to the material conditions of the 'paying' public. All over the world, governments and other higher education funders want to get a return on their investment.

They want research that is targeted at solving day-to-day material needs of society. While stargazing may help develop and harness radio and optics technology that may be applied to ground and interplanetary travel, most payers want to solve the more pressing needs of the here and now. The University has chosen the latter path. This should not be interpreted to mean that we shy away from innovation and knowledge creation, but rather that such efforts will be targeted. The University's focus areas as it seeks to exploit its rural setting are:

- Mineral and natural resource exploitation is a logical priority in a province bestowed with abundant mineral wealth and natural resources.
- Tourism flows naturally from the diverse cultural and natural heritages in the province.
- Environmental protection and sustainability while exploiting the natural resources is important for the province. In particular, water utilisation and agriculture are crucial in this regard.
- People development is paramount. We need to nurture and enhance the intellectual and operative skills of our people to enhance their quality of life away from the tedium of subsistence farming and toiling labours.

In order to realise this vision, we have re-engineered academic administration structures and academic structures. We have adopted a lean administration which should free our otherwise limited financial and human resources to concentrate on the University's core business of scholarship, research and training. In promoting and advancing the new vision, we should be mindful of the challenges facing the institution.

The first is that our rural location militates against the recruitment and retention of high quality academics. To overcome this, a number of incentives are planned which include not only financial rewards but also the beefing up of the research platform and the improvement of recreational facilities for staff and students. We have already attracted significant funding from a variety of sources; and we have created a focused Africa Research Hub to promote and co-ordinate multi-disciplinary research and community service efforts. Secondly, the University has in the past attracted students from deprived communities who have not been adequately prepared for tertiary education. To improve the situation, we have tightened up our admissions policy and are increasing our support and development systems for students and academic staff alike.

Thirdly, the challenge of financial sustainability is receiving special attention. Government subsidies are simply no longer enough. We have therefore developed a strategy to maximise the contributions from our traditional funders, while at the same time planning a structured approach to philanthropic organisations and individuals for targeted funding.

We are starting to form and nurture smart partnerships with other higher education institutions in the country, in Africa, and globally. Partnerships are also being forged with the corporate and NGO worlds and our efforts are supported by in-house systems devised to exercise tight controls on the money flowing into the University from these sources.

The merger process between the former University of the North and Medunsa is the most complex and highly charged of all the mergers. When I was appointed Interim Vice-Chancellor, I had just stabilized the Turfloop campus which for nearly a decade had been plagued with administrative and financial instability, and then faced a dysfunctional Medunsa campus. We have managed to stabilise Medunsa as well; and we are currently on the verge of solving the complex problems surrounding the establishment of the primary healthcare training site in Polokwane. The University of Limpopo is determined to build a modern and comprehensive medical training facility to bring the resultant health services and trained professionals to the people of Limpopo.

In conclusion, I have demonstrated the ability to steer this institution out of several serious crises. I have also presented a comprehensive and innovative vision that is Africa centred and rural development focused.

I have already started the implementation process which I believe I should now be given the opportunity to execute. *(As is now well known, Professor Mokgalong has been given that opportunity and the University of Limpopo).*

Chris Kanyane

Limpopo's very own medical training platform
IT'S COMING AT LAST: A FULL MEDICAL
SCHOOL IN POLOKWANE

FOR AT LEAST FIVE YEARS, THERE'S BEEN
TALK OF THE ESTABLISHMENT OF A TERTIARY
HOSPITAL AND MEDICAL SCHOOL IN LIMPOPO.
IT'S OFFICIALLY BEING CALLED A NEW
'HEALTH SCIENCES TRAINING PLATFORM'.

The in-principle decision to embark upon this development
was bound up with the complexities of the merger
between Medunsa in Gauteng and the old University
of the North. The process has been complicated by the
involvement of the National and Provincial Departments
of Education and the provincial Department of Health,
not to mention the accommodation of the various
interests in the two campuses of the merged University
of Limpopo. On the surface, sometimes, the promise of
new health and teaching facilities has seemed a distinctly
on-off affair. But this time it's definite. Key preparations
have started in earnest: the facilities are on the way.
Here are some of the basic facts. The whole project is
mandated and supported by a national cabinet decision.
A 600-bed hospital is to be built at the Edupark campus
in Polokwane. It'll be a multistorey affair so as to limit
the distance between departments.

The cost will be in the region of R1,2-billion, and the
hope is that construction will commence later this year
(2009). A detailed environmental impact study is already
under way. But there's a lot more to the project than this.
In the planning stage is the actual medical school building

and of course residential blocks for staff and students. A delegation of university and provincial personnel will be going to Australia and India soon to look at the spatial relationship between hospitals and medical schools in some of the newest developments of this kind in the world. 'We're looking for facilities here that are world class,' says Professor Peter Franks, the University's Deputy Vice-Chancellor Academic and the Turfloop campus principal. 'We're determined to make the Polokwane teaching platform the best we possibly can.'

On behalf of the Vice-Chancellor, Franks chairs the task team that has been established to co-ordinate the wide-ranging activities that are necessary to get the new facilities off the ground, as well as the teaching that needs to take place for the facilities to be fully and effectively utilised.

The task team was established at a workshop that took place last November and was attended by representatives of the University of Limpopo (from Turfloop, Medunsa and the embryonic medical campus at the Polokwane Provincial Hospital), the Limpopo Provincial Department of Health and Social Development, as well as the Limpopo Office of the Premier and Provincial Treasury. The task team appointed several key committees to facilitate the alignment of the vision of the Polokwane medical training platform with various specialized aspects of the university as a whole. These committees deal with curriculum issues, staffing requirements, logistics (including a full assessment of facilities required and a transport strategy that will link medical students with the two provincial hospitals as well as the Turfloop campus), and financial matters.

The hope is that the first medical students – probably around 50 of them, but increasing for subsequent annual intakes – will be registered at the start of 2010. Of course, the new facilities won't be ready. They'll start their studies in the science departments on the Turfloop campus and do their clinical work (from year two) in the existing Polokwane and Mankweng hospitals while the Health Sciences Training Platform is being built.

This projected 2010 commencement date is not a moment too soon for Dr Morwanphaga Nkadimeng, senior general manager of health care services in Limpopo's Department of Health. 'This country is desperate for doctors,' he asserts. 'We simply can't afford any more delays.' Nkadimeng supported his statement by pointing out that South Africa had only 20 000 doctors registered.

With the Health Professionals Council, many of whom were working overseas, and 12 000 of whom were in private practice. 'Now compare this with World Health Organisation guidelines that advise a doctor/population ratio of 1:500. Even at 50 percent of the WHO ratio, South Africa should have 45 000 doctors. But existing medical schools are producing only a thousand new doctors a year. Looked at from this perspective, the whole country is on the brink of a medical catastrophe. We in the poorer provinces are running our health services on foreign nationals. Here in Limpopo, the need is desperate.'

Franks said his steering committee was currently engaged in the preparation of a business plan for submission to the national Department of Education which will be asked to fund the Medical School facilities to the tune of up to

R1,5-billion over three years. The project is not without its difficulties, however. Nkadimeng talks forcefully about the need for the new medical school to foster relationships and linkages with top international medical universities. 'It's difficult to attract top academic staff to Polokwane,' he says; 'and the job of getting people from other countries in the south is definitely made no easier by the accreditation rules of the Health Professionals Council.

But unless we unlock these particular doors – those pertaining to international linkages and accreditation – it will be much more difficult to succeed.' Nevertheless, there is genuine enthusiasm for the Polokwane medical school project, and a determination to face the challenges that the project presents.

Franks points out that Polokwane is growing rapidly and that it will become a big regional centre over time. 'The vision of the university is to be a top-class African university solving African problems. My personal vision is that the Polokwane medical teaching platform will become a regional African resource.'

Professor Jabu Mbokazi,4 the Deputy Dean of Health Sciences who is running the embryonic medical school at Polokwane Hospital, told of a recent visit by British academic Dr John Cookson, who had helped to launch the Hull/York Medical School in north-east England five years ago. 'He was favourably impressed,' Mbokazi said. 'He admitted that the embryonic Polokwane facility was currently operating with more specialised staff than had been at it his disposal when he began with the Hull/York school.'

Professor Philip Venter, 5 the co-ordinator of the Faculty of Health Sciences on the Turfloop campus, makes no bones about his enthusiasm. 'We have huge potential here – for teaching and research,' he says. 'We're sitting right in the middle of SADC and we're in the process of getting a state-of-the-art medical school and training hospital.'

Professor Errol Holland,6 the newly appointed Executive Dean of the University's Faculty of Health Sciences, says he firmly believes that the two medical training platforms in his faculty will become world leaders in developmental medicine. 'In addition, we'll become the institution of choice for the most talented teachers and most gifted students, particularly those with noble ideals to serve the most vulnerable.'

We should allow Nkadimeng the last word. 'In 1956, a small hospital in Stellenbosch, against all the odds, became a tertiary hospital. But the will to succeed was there. Today that hospital is Tygerberg, one of South Africa's largest tertiary teaching institutions. The will to succeed – in the provincial administration and in the university – is now the most important ingredient for us.'

Mining in Limpopo: Buried treasure for Everyman?

The Turfloop Response: Occupying A special Niche

Early in 2000 a study was launched that examined the feasibility of the establishing a school of mining and minerals at the University of the North. The mandate to undertake the study emanated from a provincial mining summit held at Ellisras in 1996. The study was supported by the provincial administration, while submissions were received from relevant national departments, the corporate mining sector active in the Northern Province (now Limpopo), as well as trade unions and other mining organisations. By mid-2001 the feasibility study report had been published.

The main finding was unequivocal: a School of Mining and Minerals should be established at the University of the North to provide training and certification in the fields of mining, geology and mineral processing.

Supporting recommendations were that:
- National and provincial government agencies should assist, and local mining companies should play a supportive role;
- Mineworkers' representatives should serve on the advisory structures of the school;
- The existing Materials Modelling Centre and the Electron Microscopic Unit should form the initial research component for the school;
- R8-million be sought from the funder of the feasibility study for the first phase of the establishment of the school.

Now, three years later, considerable progress has been made. But there have been frustrations as well. The original funder, the Lebowa Mineral Trust, has since disappeared, and 'funding remains part of very lengthy and delicate negotiations'.

The words are Professor Phuti Ngoepe's. He's Turfloop's professor of physics and director of the State-of-the-art Materials Modelling Centre housed within the University's School of Physical and Mineral Sciences. Ngoepe was the original chairman of the School of Mining and Minerals feasibility project, and he remains closely involved.

'The province has identified mining as one of its three major economic pillars, and has accordingly prioritised the development of a platinum cluster and a chemical cluster based on coal,' he says. 'These provincial goals – not to mention the national and broader African goals with regard to mining and downstream beneficiation – present an enormous challenge to UNIN in finding its proper place relative to this sector.' Ngoepe's perceptions of this 'proper place' are straightforward.

The University is ideally located in the middle of Limpopo – at once the epicentre of South Africa's newest mining activities AND the country's most rural province – to take a leading role in the development of mining activity and expertise that benefits previously excluded people and communities.

This is where the Mining Charter fits in, of course – and a new concept referred to as 'junior mining'. This is really an attempt to open up a traditionally capital intensive industry, the preserve of large corporations, to smaller local companies and entrepreneurs.

As Ngoepe says: 'Exciting opportunities exist for black economic empowerment, especially in the junior mining sector. These emerging mining entrepreneurs are facing enormous challenges, whether in raising capital, mining exploration, acquisition and use of appropriate equipment and technologies, environmental rehabilitation, processing, innovation and marketing – and human resource development as a whole. Turfloop must now view the junior mining sector as its most meaningful niche area.' Ngoepe refers to several recent comments made by senior provincial and national officials from several different government departments as clear indications of what is being expected from Turfloop. 'History will judge us harshly,' he says, 'if we don't act with vigour now to fully occupy this niche.'

Let's see what has been done at the University so far. For a start, there's the Mining Certificate Course, launched in 2002 with 19 students, which to date has provided new opportunities for around 300 graduates. This month-long course takes students through an introduction to geology, mining law, mining operations and safety, as well as environmental protection.

Still in the pipeline is six month diploma and advanced diploma courses in mining. Three-way collaboration in this regard is well advanced between UNIN, the School of Mines in Bulawayo, Zimbabwe, and two institutions in Canada (Queens University and Cambrian College). Both the Canadian institutions specialise in mining, and have wide experience of working in Africa, having helped to establish the Bulawayo School of Mines and also being involved in mining-related training initiatives in Tanzania, Zambia and Malawi. A Canadian diploma course already exists, and work is under way to modify it to local conditions, to the Mining Charter, and to the demands of the National Qualifications Framework.

Full BSc degrees are also planned. These will specialise in practical mining, geology and minerology. A post-graduate programme already offers law students the opportunity to do a Master's degree in environmental and mining law. On the research side, Turfloop's growth and capacity built over the past ten years is impressive.

Complex activities related to mineral properties and processing are being carried out. In particular, the computer modeling of minerals and alloys is undertaken in partnership with mining houses and research bodies. Previously, materials were physically tested. Now, computer modelling speeds up the testing process and cuts costs by making computer predictions based on the atomic structure of the materials.

The University's Materials Modelling Centre is the only centre in South African higher education where computer modelling is conducted on materials for industrial applications. The Royal Society in Britain helped to set up the Modelling Centre in partnership with the South African National Research Foundation. A Royal Society spokesperson said recently: 'The University's Materials Modelling Centre has a momentum of its own and is competitive at the international level. The natural ability we met [at Turfloop] was very good. Here is a big catchment area of people capable of high achievement. If the historically disadvantaged universities are to succeed, they must have some research programmes and people at the forefront of knowledge.'

The Centre's high-tech modelling procedures have helped towards understanding the properties of platinum-based alloys, and details relating to platinum-group metals separation and beneficiation. All this is essential in increasing the value of Limpopo's mineral resources and offers an essential service to the country's mining and manufacturing industries.

During a recent visit to Canada, says Ngoepe, Turfloop academics were 'sensitised to the value of virtual reality tools in the field of mining'. 'One of the potential areas of cooperation with universities in Canada will be in establishing a virtual reality centre at Turfloop. This will provide three-dimensional visualisation to assist with exploration, evaluation of ore deposits, mining design, safety and health issues, and environmental protection and rehabilitation.'

All this – and a lot more – provides a solid research component for Turfloop's mooted School of Minerals and Mining. 'It's very exciting,' Ngoepe concludes, 'to have all this technology to assist us as we push forward with the Mining Charter and the active support of the concept of junior mining.'

Powerful new university leadership

Dr Reuel Khoza – Committed, not merely nominal

A Junior psychology lecturer and postgraduate student who lost his job for political activism in 1974 has now become the Chancellor of His Alma Mater. He is the first Chancellor to be appointed since the old University of the North and the Medical University of Southern Africa (Medunsa) merged into a single institution on 1 January 2005.

Dr Reuel Khoza was inaugurated on the 9 November 2007. He is an apt and dynamic choice for a University that has as its stated vision: "to be a leading African University, epitomizing excellence and global competitiveness" and to concern itself on the teaching and research side with "finding solutions for Africa".

If you doubt his suitability, then listen to a brief description of Dr Khoza. He is a highly successful businessman; he is an Africanist; he is a change agent in the forefront of black economic empowerment. He is currently chairman and major shareholder of Aka Capital, a private equity company. He is also chairman of corobrik, Nedbank Limited, Nedbank Group, Murray & Roberts Cementation and the Nepad Business Foundation. On top of all this, he is the president of the Institute of Directors in South Africa, and he holds directorships on the boards of Protea Hospitality Limited, Nampak, and Old Mutual plc. He is also on the Presidential Economic Advisory Panel, and a member (and past director and patron) of the Black Management Forum.

The list of the achievements of this 59 year old South African is hugely impressive. He exudes energy and commitment. He says of his alma mater "I have no interest in being merely a nominal or ceremonial Chancellor. I am concerned and I want to contribute – particularly in helping to develop existing and potential centres of excellence on both campuses"

He speaks impressively of his concerns over Africa, and of his vision for the continent. In his inaugural address last year he made specific reference to the university's motto:

Providing Solutions for Africa. This means, he declared, that "our stance is clear. We purposely and emphatically refuse to be conditioned by circumstances imposed by a past of slavery, colonialism, neo-colonialism, racism and apartheid. We choose, instead, to create a new world characterized by the rule of law, human rights, socio-economic development and prosperity. We shall be masters and mistresses of our own destiny... marching to our own brisk rhythm as we take on a rapidly globalizing and fiercely competitive world"

But Khoza warned several dangers that might obstruct such a vision. The first was the danger of being so proundly African that knowledge coming from "a heritage we could not claim as our own" was sometimes rejected. "It matters not what the ideological slant of the knowledge is; it matters not if we cannot claim the knowledge as being part of our intellectual heritage. What matters is the purpose to which the knowledge is put".

What is the best possible purpose for the University of Limpopo? "Our vision" says Khoza, "should be to put our educational efforts towards achieving an African Renaissance. And what is this Renaissance but the realization of a people that they can be masters of their on destiny."

The second danger against which Khoza warned was what he called the "victim mentality" which is often prevalent in Africa today, and not least in South Africa. "the realization and belief that one is the master of one's own destiny, whether as an individual or a people, is called a sense of efficacy. Lacking a sense of efficacy means that as a people we consider ourselves subject to elements; subject to fate; subject to the will of others; subject to providence. A culture of dependency develops in such a people: a culture of no achievement, a culture of no self esteem, no dignity, no pride.

"Thus we observe people who seek and expect handouts, donations, alms at every opportunity. We observe people who seek survival and prosperity by stealing and looting. We observe people who expect to be taught rather than to learn. We see people who have perfected the art of blame. They blame colonialism, they blame imperialism, they blame apartheid, they blame God".

Khoza makes mention of the strides made in the Far East and Pacific Rim when knowledge and the technology from other sources were actively sought out and embraced. "By contrast, the African approach has been to quibble about the Afrocentricity or Eurocentricity of knowledge… But education for African Renaissance must reject this view. It must recognize that in education there is no shame in borrowing from those who have travelled the road before you. In fact, the core of education is learning more from the experience of others than from one's own experience".

The author of these challenging concepts was born in Acornhoek, a deep rural area not far from the Kruger National Park. He went to school in Tzaneen and Bushbuckridge, matriculating in 1969. At the University of the North he did bachelors and honours degrees in psychology. During his postgraduate years he worked as junior lecturer and research officer. And it was at this time that he got into trouble with the University authorities.

"I had to become the president of the Psychology Society on campus, and I as also the chairman of the University Choral Society. I used both these platforms to become politically vocal. My choice of songs – their political messages – particularly irritated the authorities. Finally, at the time of the Frelimo rallies in 1974 and after some bad reports from security branch agents – we called them sinister beasts – on campus, I as asked to leave".

But this setback Khoza turned to his own advantage. He took a job with Unilever and rapidly rose to the position of a brand manager. In 1978 he successfully applied for a Shell scholarship to study in Britain. He returned a year later with a Masters in Marketing Management from the University of Lancaster. After a two year stint with Shell, he started his own management consulting company that grew over the next 16 years into his personal foothold in the world of business. In 2005, he achieved an Engineering Doctorate (Business) from the University of Warwick in the University of United Kingdom.

And earlier this year he received an honorary doctorate in recognition of "a visionary African humanist whose outlook and life's work has been informed by a strong sense of integrity, by a humble style of leadership, and by committed service to his country".

Speaking again of Africa and the role that the University of Limpopo could play in it, Khoza explains that the world was diverging as the developed countries continued to outstrip the developing ones. "Yet at the same time there is a powerful convergence: the world is a global village. My sense is this: if Africa can take advantage of all the technological aids to learning that are becoming available today, the continent can leapfrog itself into the 21st century. That is the real challenge facing the continent – and our University – today.

"The imperative, then, is that we pursue excellence – aggressively and actively. I would like to work with the University, looking first at the funding and creation of a comprehensive chair of mining engineering. We should be doing nothing less because of our position in the world's richest platinum basin. By "a comprehensive chair", I mean not only one professorial chair, but surrounding that chair with other professorial and lecturing positions, research posts, and of course the equipment and infrastructure necessary to make the potential really fly".

000 The End 000

References

Acknowledgements and List of Sources Consulted

Turfloop testimony: the dilemma of a black university in South Africa / edited by G. M. Nkondo: Raven Press

The Concept of a University / Kenneth Minogue: Transaction Publishers

Within the Realm of Possibility: From Disadvantage to Development at the University of Fort Hare and the University of the North / edited by *Mokubung Nkomo, Derrick Swartz, Botshabelo Maja (eds): HSRC Press* (For the information that was used from a chapter written by Prof FitzGerald entitled Intrepreneurial and entrepreneurial developments at the University of the North)

Definition of Black Consciousness / Azanian People Organization: www.Azapo.org.za

Biography of Onkgopotse Abram Tiro / South African History Online: *Rewriting history, critically examining our past, strengthening the teaching of history:* <u>*www.sahistory.org.za*</u>

United Democratic Front / African History Online: Rewriting history, *critically examining our past, strengthening the teaching of history*

"Beyond Our Wildest Dreams": The United Democratic Front and the Transformation of South Africa / Ineke van Kessel: University of Virginia Press

Opposing apartheid / University of Connecticut: www. uconn.edu